CAST NET
— M A S T E R Y —

Captain Michael Grimm
Companion Site: www.LiveBait.com

Printed in the United States of America
First Printing 2020
First Edition 2020

ISBN: 9798636420712

<u>Disclaimer</u>

CAST NET

— M A S T E R Y —

How the Best Fishermen "Make Bait" & Catch More Fish

Captain Michael Grimm

TABLE OF CONTENTS

PREFACE

Do you want to catch more fish? Of course you do. We all do. I'm Captain Mike. I excelled first as a Recreational Angler and then as a Captain by developing and honing my own techniques with the guidance of some of the best live bait fishermen in the world. Never once have I stopped seeking a better way to catch more fish. If you're not getting better, you're getting worse. I worked hard, asked questions, tried new tactics, observed and studied my results to establish the high-level techniques that I use on a daily basis.

And now, I will share them with you so that YOU can also benefit from my obsession.

I am not one of those "zero sum" captains that view other anglers as a threat to my livelihood. There are some on the water who believe that their business thrives so long as anglers don't expand and improve their angling skills. Not me. It is my life's joy to see you catch more fish and create more memories. Exceptional anglers helped me along early in my career and I want to help YOU in the same way. I believe in the maxim that a "rising tide floats all boats."

For me, my angling success ascended to another level when I dedicated myself to the art of catching all sorts of LIVE BAIT.

It's that simple. Mastering the art of cast netting over my thirty-five-year fishing career has enabled me to catch live bait when others cannot.

The best piece of advice I can give to anglers of all ages and experience levels is: Use LIVE BAIT.

Catching your own live bait results in catching more fish and bigger fish.

After years of fishing with clients and friends, being approached at events from iCAST to boat shows, answering more e-mails, private messages and Youtube comments than I can count, it was apparent that I needed to write this book.

Through seminars, demonstrations and online videos, I have taught thousands of anglers how to use a cast net. It is my desire to help those who are eager to improve and expand their fishing skills. It gives me great pleasure to share my life's passion through teaching and instruction, not to mention that with every lesson, I am further able to hone my own skillset!

Getting kids to shut off video game consoles, putting down the cell phones and encouraging them to go outdoors gives me satisfaction as well. I get a big kick out of seeing parents bond with their children while learning something new and enjoying the outdoors—like I did with my father.

With my Mastery Series, I can't wait to share with you everything that I've learned from countless hours of trial and error as well as tips from mentors, professional captains and some of the industry's elite. I will teach you everything you need to become a better fisherman by taking full advantage of your cast net. I'm not holding back. You get it all.

By the time you finish this book, not only will you be able to open a cast net in a perfect circle and "make bait" but you will join the "90/10" fishing club. That's right. The other 90% of anglers will envy you and wonder what you are doing differently. Simply put, fishing is about to get a whole lot easier for you.

"10% of fishermen catch 90% of the fish"

THE 90/10 FISHING CLUB

For average fishermen, fishing is merely a pastime or a hobby. It is an opportunity to get outdoors, share time with family, reflect on life or simply soak in a bit of solitude. Whether they catch something or not, it's not important. The journey and adventure that comes with fishing are more than enough to make the trip worthwhile. You'll hear them say things like, "Well, that's fishing", "It's great to just get out on the water" or "Should have been here yesterday", when they come back to the dock empty-handed. This is the 90% Club. Are you content to be a member of this club? Let's hope not.

On the other hand, there are anglers who treat fishing as a lifestyle or even a mission. There are those who are driven to excel and to challenge themselves to be able to catch the biggest fish on the lightest tackle and to target the species of their choosing – and do it all CONSISTENTLY. Don't bother telling these anglers about "Luck." They MAKE their own Luck. This is why 10% of fishermen catch 90% of the fish - and 10% may be a generous estimate.

Those of us in the *10% Club* aren't seeking "relaxation." We enjoy the satisfaction and accomplishment of consistently catching what we set out to catch. We're also a very competitive bunch. If we weren't, there'd be no such things as fishing tournaments.

While anglers in the *10% Club* value and share certain traits, the ability to "make bait" is one of the most highly-prized. You'll hear me refer to these fishermen as the "ten percenters" throughout this Mastery Series.

Starting right now, it's my mission to get you CONSISTENTLY catching bait with your cast net. The mere fact that you are reading this tells me that you are thirsting to learn and improve, and that you are ten percenter material.

To make bait -

Catching bait fish by oneself.

INTRODUCTION
MY STORY

S ome of my peers believe that I started out catching bait from my crib. If only that were true.

Growing up, some of my fondest memories were learning how to catch my own bait. More specifically, learning to throw a cast net and getting really good at it. I like to say, "When you can catch bait, the fishing is easy."

My first cast net was a three-footer that my dad bought me at the tender age of five. To toss the net, I would put the net in my teeth and chuck it on the lawn in a near-perfect circle. Getting outdoors with the salt breeze on my face and the anticipation of catching fish made me one happy little fisherman. I had "the fever" and the only "cure" was to be on the water.

As I grew older, I graduated to larger and heavier cast nets. Watching the commercial bait fishermen "pancake" fourteen-foot cast nets was something I would gawk at all day. I couldn't take my eyes off them until they pulled up their nets loaded with tons of flickering bait. It was more exciting than actually catching fish – and I wanted to be just like them!

Although I wasn't a big kid by any means, about five-foot-ten and skinny, I was determined to throw bigger nets like the pros. I moved up to a six-foot net and, soon after, bought my first ten-foot cast net sometime around sixteen years old. It was a big investment for me. I just remember that net being a beast and weighed a ton. I thought I had made a HUGE mistake.

I practiced on the lawn in the heat of the summer until I was drenched in sweat, losing weight I couldn't afford to lose. The only instruction I had was a folded piece of paper, seemingly from the 1950s, with a few caveman drawings. Brutal! Try learning how to throw a cast net from reading a Peanuts comic strip. Keep in mind that there was no YouTube or video series to demonstrate the proper way to effectively open that beast. I was frustrated and ready to revert back to my six-footer.

Luckily, I had that one friend who could really open a cast net to show me the way. Now, I'm that friend to YOU.

My friend was taller and bigger than me. I wasn't sure if I could even get the net open like he did, but I had to try! I asked him how he opened his net so effortlessly. And, you guessed it, he was reluctant to show me his "secret sauce." For all I knew, he had spent hours on end perfecting his top-secret method. He was a big physics nerd too. I felt like I was asking him to reveal his top-secret fishing spot. I demonstrated my technique by holding the cast net in my teeth and whirling around in a crazy spin. I could open the ten-footer about seventy percent or so, swinging it like a wild man to get momentum. It was far from an effortless technique as I clenched my teeth and held my breath. I was so embarrassed. I think he felt bad for me.

He immediately grabbed my net and loaded it over his shoulder. He fanned the net like I've seen the commercial bait guys do. He was going so fast I couldn't keep up. I was excited but nervous as I watched and studied every movement.

And boom! He opened the most beautiful "pancake" right on the lawn in front of me! It was almost as if in slow motion when the net left his hands. It looked effortless! The close part of the net hit the ground first, and the rest of the net just laid out in a perfect circle, lead by lead. It was so beautiful!

We looked at each other. He tossed the handline to me and said, "There! Now you try." My heart was racing. I wasn't sure how the heck he did it. By the way, he was captain of the football team too!

I picked up the cast net, coiled the handline and nervously began trying to mimic his motions. He stopped me and, like a father showing his son how to throw a baseball for the first time, walked me through his entire "top-secret" method.

He loaded it in my hand and over my shoulder perfectly. He explained everything thoroughly. He was an amazing teacher! Suddenly, the net wasn't as heavy. It could have partly been my surging adrenaline or the anxiety attack I was having, but knowing what I know now, it was all technique. He loaded the net for me into three pieces, distributing the weight over my slender body. He explained to me that the net was "already open – just let the leads do the work." I wound up the net as instructed and, to my amazement, the net exploded into a perfect circle.

It was the most incredible feeling of my young life—aside from a three-pointer I hit at the buzzer in a summer basketball league (we only needed two points to win).

I thanked my buddy and he left. After he left, I practiced until I nearly collapsed from exhaustion. From that day forward, my ten-foot cast net went everywhere I went and I would go on to hone my skill, day after day.

I remember the first time I pancaked the net over a school of pilchards. I couldn't even drag the loaded cast net over the gunnels. It was jam-packed and I felt just like a commercial bait fisherman at that moment.

I loaded the boat with about two hundred fresh, frisky pilchards. It was an incredible feeling. This was a pivotal moment - a true game-changer - in my fishing career that put me one step closer to the 10% club. I'll say it again: "10% of all fishermen catch 90% of the fish."

That quote couldn't be more applicable and that's where I want YOU to be.

A Captain's Advice on Catching More Fish:

"Learn how to catch bait and the fishing is easy."

Captain Mike

CHAPTER 1
MAKE BAIT

History of Cast Netting

Cast nets are thought to have been created in the 4th century, possibly 301 AD! The ancient Polynesians most likely used the nets after settling in Hawaii around that time. Historians have discovered ancient pottery with illustrations of fishermen weaving and casting nets. They were first made using linen and cotton.

The Polynesians didn't use the nets just to catch bait, though. They used the nets to catch FOOD and they were quite adept at it! Cast net fishing soon became very popular on the big island and, ultimately, around the world as explorers and wayfarers visited the Hawaiian Islands and returned home with stories of catching fish with these amazing nets.

Why Cast Nets Are Used

Baitfish such as mullet are considered vegetarian, hence why cast nets were constructed. Recreational fishermen utilize cast nets as a sustainable way to catch baitfish since the nets are limited to a certain size by regulation or statute.

Cast nets can be opened by one person and yield several baitfish that can be used to catch large predatory game fish ranging from Largemouth Bass to Mahi Mahi – and everything in between. All game fish eat smaller fish, so having the ability to catch baitfish is essential! You can bet that the majority of the *ten percenters* know how to open a cast net to catch their own live bait, and they are very, very good at it.

By being able to "make bait," you stack the odds in your favor. With all due respect to you fly fishermen out there, there is no better presentation than a freshly caught live bait placed in front of a hungry game fish. You've heard the saying "Match the Hatch", right? It means simply offering predators exactly what they are eating. The ten percenters always know what the targeted fish are eating and that's the bait they will use to get bites.

For example, during the fall mullet run migration down the Florida coast, Tarpon are feasting on massive pods of mullet as the mullet make their way south along the beaches and coastline, taking refuge in numbers. Fishing for tarpon with anything other than mullet would be absolutely foolish. So, too, when in the late winter, Tarpon switch to feeding on shrimp and then, in the spring, on crabs, etc. Only the *ten percenters* know all this. It's about time that you did, too.

The day of a *ten percenter* starts with catching fresh live bait and ends with catching trophy game fish.

Cast nets are also used to support conservation efforts by capturing fish for research without harming them. Researchers then use these fish to study populations and analyze species data of the surrounding fisheries.

Regulations: While cast nets promote a sustainable fishery, they still must be regulated. Each State, County and even municipality enforces their own set of regulations. For example, here in Miami we can throw up to a fourteen-foot (radius) cast net, but in New York you can only throw up to a ten-footer as a recreational angler.

Would you believe cast nets are completely illegal in the inland waters of California? It's true.

Visit LiveBait.com to find out the cast net regulations for where you are fishing before purchasing a net.

The Best Bait is Fresh Bait

Before I became a *ten percenter*, I had no clue about live bait and how it would drastically change the way I fished. I would go bass fishing in local lakes with lures and offshore trolling the deep blue sea with dead bait such as ballyhoo. And there is nothing wrong with either method.

While I would do pretty well with the bass, the offshore fishing trips were underwhelming and the people I fished with just accepted it as bad luck with "hey, that's fishing." Well, not me! I knew that I could do better!

During my sophomore year of high school, I met another soon-to-be lifelong friend, Matthew Bogle. He introduced me to live bait fishing the offshore waters of South Florida.

I had passed by Matt in our high school hallways and had also seen him aboard his 13' Boston Whaler in the same marina where my Dad kept his sailboat moored. Matt always wore fishing shirts emblazoned with jumping Mahi or Sailfish. Something told me that this guy was legit.

Every square inch of his small boat was crammed with fishing rods, outriggers - and a cooler he used as a livewell. I couldn't take my eyes off him as he idled to the main channel and then out to the deep blue sea. I just knew that Matt would be catching something big. I also knew that I was missing out!

During my high school years, every kid – including me - dreamed of owning a Boston Whaler – and this kid was living MY dream! If you are old enough to remember the 60s TV show "Flipper", that was Matt's life. And all I could do was dream about it and work hard in hopes of getting there too.

It wasn't long before our paths crossed. As fate would have it, we had marine biology class together. On a field trip, I was lucky enough to sit next to

Matt on the bus. We immediately started talking. He loved to fish! We discussed boats, fishing and heading to some islands in the Bahamas.

I was fascinated – and a bit jealous – at how Matt was catching Mahi Mahi consistently! Mahi were my dream fish. Something I could catch and eat? Sign me up! Sadly, Matt's little Whaler only had room for two and he already had a fishing buddy. So, I waited patiently, studying fishing magazines and perfecting my cast netting skills.

Then, "the day" arrived. I finally got the invite I had been waiting for! Matt sold his 13' Boston Whaler and upgraded to something a bit more seaworthy: a 20' center console. I met Matt at his house on a winter morning, hours before daybreak. He backed his Ford Explorer up to the boat trailer and off we went. Even though he was only seventeen, Matt towed that five-thousand-pound rig like a pro! He even had a cup of coffee on his dash and looked like he needed a shave.

We launched Matt's boat and made our way "out front." What was the first order of business? MAKE BAIT!

In the stern of Matt's new boat sat a plastic storage bin bought at Walmart with a hole drilled into the bottom for water inflow. At the top was a fitting for an overflow. The thing was flimsy, but it worked great! The design was simple but effective.

Once we arrived at the inlet, Matt used his "Hummingbird" fish finder to lock in on the pilchards using sonar. Another first for me! He showed me what bait looked like on the screen and instructed me to let him know whenever the bait ball appeared on the display.

Instead of using a cast net, Matt caught pilchards with a Sabiki rig using a rod and reel. He set me up with a rig too. The weather was cold and I was piercing my fingers with the sharp hooks, but I was having a blast. We were pulling up six beautiful baits at a time, loading the livewell in short order. Between the two of us, we managed about ten dozen freshly-caught pilchards. That is what I call "**Making Bait**".

We then headed about three miles due east and then south to a popular spot called the "Stink Hole." It was some sort of underwater water treatment discharge. (Don't ask.) It was choppy too and my sea legs were to be tested.

Once we arrived in the area, we could see the water was different, sort of bubbly. He took out his anchor and tossed it nearby allowing the boat to sit perfectly up-current. At the time, I had no clue of just how precise and calculated Matt was.

Matt broke out some wire and twisted leaders together so that we could target "toothy" Kingfish. He'd find swivels and hooks hidden in the deck gutters from his previous trips to finish off his rigs perfectly. He was in no rush as he studied the surrounding conditions by watching the birds and life around the boat. Very deliberate. He even had a hand-held GPS to identify underwater wrecks and areas where he previously caught fish.

We soon deployed two flat lines (meaning no floats or weights) with fresh pilchards, rigged with wire leader and treble hooks. He then put up a fishing kite with a single bait on the surface. Matt was a rock star! All I could do was watch and stay out of his way.

He took a scoop of bait in his hand and tossed it in the air behind the boat. I was getting my first taste of live chumming. It wasn't long before Kingfish were skyrocketing after our baits, and Fish On! The sweet sound of those old Daiwa BG 90's screaming drag was thrilling! I can still hear them now.

I had never caught a kingfish before, but that day I caught Kingfish, Mahi, Sailfish, and Blackfin Tuna! At that moment, I knew that LIVE BAIT was KING and an UNFAIR ADVANTAGE!

Matt became a lifelong fishing buddy and, believe it or not, he wasn't the best cast net fisherman. He actually struggled from lack of experience as the baits were just too deep for a cast net where we were fishing.

One day with Matt, I caught a glimpse of a school of mullet at the boat ramp when we were launching. I broke out my ten-foot cast net and fired off a perfect pancake right in his face! Matt was impressed but played it off. After all, HE was the teacher and I was the pupil.

From that day forward, I always brought my cast net aboard. On the days we couldn't catch pilchards with Sabikis, I would cast net fresh ballyhoo on the reef. He would rely on me to make perfect tosses with my cast net and load up on bait. We were a team. And we created some of the best memories of my life. **I never went fishing without live bait again.**

Check out this 64-pound kingfish we caught using a live blue runner back in 1999. Do you think we could have caught that fish using dead bait or lures? Probably not. Live bait is the easiest way to catch fish and I will teach you how using cast net will vastly improve your success rate.

How Cast Nets Can Improve Your Fishing Success

I get asked all the time, "Captain Mike, how can I catch more fish?" My answer is always the same: "USE LIVE BAIT." It is the best advice I can give to aspiring anglers. If you can't catch live bait on your own, then buy it. Fishing with live bait is the most natural and effective presentation there is in fishing.

Catching your own live bait is a significant advantage in fishing and, to do so, you will need to become GREAT with your cast net. Being able to catch your own live bait also puts you firmly in control of the success of your trips. No more worrying about whether the "bait guy" is sold out or whether he sells you weak, tired baits. Once you can load your livewells full of fresh live bait, you will have no problem catching more fish. Trust me.

Some days when you're fishing offshore, a Mahi Mahi will likely eat just about anything you can pitch to them, but on the days when they are finicky, pitch a fresh, juicy live bait in front of one – especially the bigger Mahi - and it will be hard for it to resist.

Before I put a cast net in your hand and show you how to open a perfect "pancake," you must first understand the fundamentals. Let's get started.

CHAPTER 2
CAST NET FUNDAMENTALS

What is a Cast Net?

A cast net is a circular net, typically constructed of monofilament mesh, that is designed to be thrown by one person. It opens in the air, lands on the water, and sinks over the targeted baitfish. When the fish are inside the net, the fisherman can close it by pulling the handline to close the drawstrings attached to the lead line. The fish get trapped inside the net as this motion forms a bag and prevents their escape.

Cast nets are great fishing tools for recreational anglers to minimize their impact to a given fishery. Cast nets are small enough to be handled by one person yet big enough to catch non-game fish used for bait. Mammals such as turtles are not harmed like they are in large commercial net fishing. Any by-catch caught by cast nets can be safely released simply by opening the net.

Typically, anglers use cast nets to catch bait such as mullet, bunker, shrimp, pilchards, shad, sardines, ballyhoo, croakers, shiners and the list goes on. Cast nets work equally well in saltwater, freshwater, rivers, bays, lakes, and oceans. It is one of the best tackle investments you can make.

Anatomy of a Cast Net

Just about every cast net shares the same design elements. However, the quality of the components used to build the net will vary. A cast net's components should include a handline, horn, braille lines, and lead line.

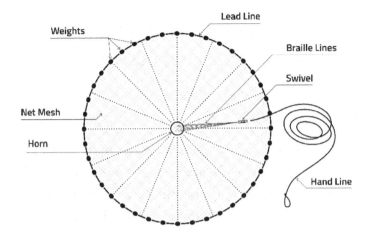

A premium, high-performance cast net such as a JuJu cast net will feature techniques only found in hand-made cast net construction. Premium nets feature a hand-tied, six-panel design that makes the net far easier to open into a full, flat circle to maximize each throw. This means there are six pie-shaped pieces tied together to form a perfect circle.

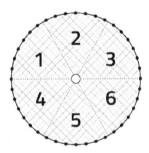

Do yourself a favor and invest in a premium cast net. The results will be far more satisfying. Your net should also last longer. Once you take catching live bait seriously, you are one step closer to joining the *ten percenters.*

Those already in the *ten percent club* would never own a poorly-constructed net. It's about maximizing your catch and to do so, you'll need a well-made cast net.

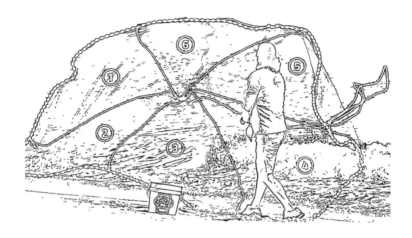

Materials of a Cast Net

Most cast nets are constructed using monofilament line. The thickness of the line depends on the mesh size of the net. A quality net uses soft mesh and heavy-duty braille lines.

In the past, most cast nets were made of nylon instead of monofilament. Nylon was developed around the mid-nineteenth century and used as a new material in the construction of cast nets. There are still some nylon nets available on the market, although I don't recommend them as they don't sink as fast and they are more visible to baitfish. Being stealthy in cast net fishing is as equally important as with rod and reel fishing. These are truly "old school" nets because monofilament manufacturing techniques were not quite mature 40+ years ago.

Length of a Cast Net

When you purchase a cast net, you will notice that all nets are labeled by a radius of three to fourteen feet. This number is half the size of the full diameter. For example, a ten-foot cast net opens to a diameter of twenty feet, a four-footer opens to eight, and so on.

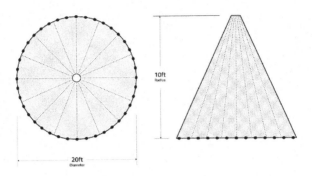

Don't make the common mistake of purchasing the wrong-sized cast net. Each state has its own size regulations, so first check the regulations where you are fishing to ensure you are buying a legal net.

For example, the state of Texas allows up to a fourteen-foot diameter cast net. The keyword here is "diameter." Anglers will often go to their local tackle store and purchase a fourteen-footer, not realizing that "fourteen" is only half the size of the net. A cast net on the shelf marketed as fourteen-foot opens to a twenty-eight-foot diameter, making it illegal in the state of Texas. The correct cast net to buy in this case would be a seven-footer, which opens to the maximum legal size of a fourteen-foot diameter.

Remember: A Cast Net is identified by its radius.

Before you purchase your first net, check the regulations. I've compiled a list of regulations for you available at LiveBait.com.

Cast Net Components

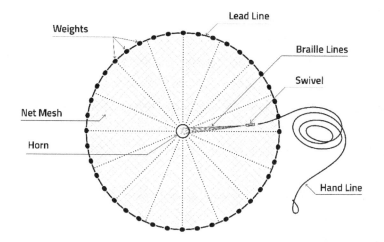

Handline

With each cast net comes a Handline that you will place around your wrist. (The Handline is rather helpful…if you want your net back after the first cast.) The Handline is used to retrieve and close your net to bring in your catch. A quality cast net might include up to 30' of heavy-duty poly-braided floating or nylon line. This allows you to throw your cast net into deeper water as well as off bridges and piers.

Horn

The **Horn** of a cast net is at the very top of the net, connected to the **Selvage**. You will use the horn by pulling up on it to open the cast net, allowing you to unload your fresh catch.

In the past, the horn was made out of sections of steer horn, hence the name. Today, horns are made using heavy duty plastic and come in a variety of sizes. There are several different types of horns, and I have used them all. I prefer a large and open horn without cross-sections. This allows you to clear your braille line or tangles easily. If you were to get bait or seaweed stuck in the horn, it is easier to remove.

Mesh

Mesh size is the measurement of the squares from knot to knot in the webbing of the net. Mesh size should be your primary consideration when purchasing a cast net.

The most common mesh sizes include 3/16", 1/4", 3/8", 1/2", 5/8," and 1." The size of the baitfish you are targeting will determine which size mesh works best. This is because you don't want your baits to "gill" themselves in a mesh that is too big.

Worse yet, you don't want the baits escaping through mesh that is too big. You must balance the mesh size against getting the maximum sink rate.

As a rule of thumb, 3/8" is a great all-purpose mesh that can be used to catch different size baits between 3" and 12." On any given day, I use a 3/8" mesh net to catch big pilchards, mullet of all sizes, pinfish and ballyhoo. It's nearly limitless what I can catch with that mesh size.

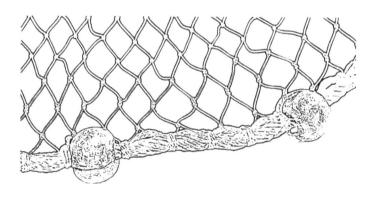

In the chart below, I match each mesh to a targeted baitfish.

Bait/mesh size chart:

Mesh Size	Bait Size	Bait Fish
3/16"	1" to 2"	Glass Minnows, Anchovy, Grass Shrimp
1/4"	1" to 3"	Small Pilchards, Sardines, Threadfins
3/8" (All Purpose)	3" and Up	Medium Pilchards, Sardines, Threadfins, Pinfish
1/2"	6" and Up	Large Pilchards, Sardines, Threadfins, Ballyhoo, Pinfish
5/8"	8" and Up	Menhaden, Blue Runners, Speedos, Medium Mullet
1"	10" and Up	Medium to Large Mullet
1 1/8"	10" and Up	Large Mullet

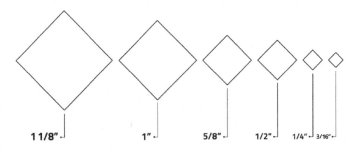

Braille lines

The **Braille** lines are the lines of monofilament that run directly through the horn attached to a swivel and down to your lead line. (Some call these the "draw strings.") By pulling the braille lines to you, you close the cast net, forming a closed bag. Higher-quality cast nets will have more braille lines closing the net faster, not allowing bait to escape.

In a poor-quality net, you will find far fewer braille lines attached to the lead line, exposing too many openings for baits to wriggle free.

Mullet are notorious for finding the gaps between the leads to escape to freedom. Later in this Mastery Course, I will teach you how to close the net properly to prevent your cherished baits from escaping.

Swivel

The **Swivel** that connects the handline to the braille lines is often overlooked, yet it is very important. I always look at the swivel type and craftsmanship of the connection. When I'm evaluating a cast net, the quality of the swivel and connection is a good indication of whether the cast net is a premium net.

JuJu cast nets are made with a robust, commercial-grade inline swivel that is stronger and lasts longer than typical swivels. The swivel is hand-tied to the braille lines rather than using a crimp that could get caught in your mesh and cause tangles.

A poor-quality swivel or connection will result in more twists and make it difficult to open full circles with your cast net. You'll see me refer to "pancakes" repeatedly in this Mastery Series.

In order to achieve a full "pancake," the construction of the net and its components are very important.

Selvage

The point at which the net is connected to the horn and lead line is called the **Selvage**. This is the point of the highest stress placed on the cast net. This is also the most likely component to give out on poor-quality nets.

The method used to attach the net to the horn varies by manufacturer. A premium cast net is a work of art in this regard, so pay close attention to the selvage when selecting a net.

On some nets, you may see double Selvage. I prefer double selvage on the ten-foot specialty cast net I use for mullet. Mullet are large and often take refuge in rocky areas. The double line helps prevent tears and prolongs the lifespan of the net.

I have personally stress-tested nets to improve the selvage. I've found that a double selvage isn't needed by most live bait fishermen.

However, the double selvage seems to be the trend in cast net construction to entice anglers to buy the nets.

Remember: Buy a cast net that catches fish - not fishermen.

Lead line

The **lead line** rings the bottom of the net, which is the first part of your net to hit the water. The lead line is made up of weights (also called "leads" – pronounced like "led") that causes your cast net to sink through the water column, thereby trapping bait in your net. A quality lead line is very important to your success in cast netting. High-performance cast nets feature spherical, marble-sized leads spaced about two inches apart. The marble shape reduces tangles and, by being close together, the bait is less likely to escape. This shape is also a hydrodynamic shape that sinks with minimum resistance.

A Bucket is Not Just a Bucket

Most cast nets are packaged within a small box or bucket. I prefer a 3.5-gallon bucket to a standard 5-gallon bucket because the smaller bucket is easier to store and fits within the hatches of my boat, under seats, etc. These buckets come in handy for many aspects of fishing such as holding live bait, storing tackle, using for a wash down, cleaning and a toilet.

The small plastic boxes used as cast net packaging that you typically see in stores are essentially useless. Good luck even getting your net to fit back into the box after the first use. These boxes were simply made to save space on store shelves - not to provide anglers with a multi-purpose accessory.

Getting the most use out your bucket will keep you organized and one step closer to the *ten-percent club*.

The best fishermen are well-organized. From buckets to tackle trays, everything is in perfect order. This reminds me of when I took up golf and one pro commented on the organization of my golf bag. He wasn't impressed and told me that he would never see the pros walk around the course without perfect harmony in their golf bags.

This is how the *ten-percent club* operates and you're getting there. But first, let's learn the physics of cast netting which are very important to understand in your journey to cast net mastery.

CHAPTER 3
PHYSICS OF CAST NETTING

Small Net vs. Big Net

Would you believe that a big cast net is easier to throw than a small net? It's true! Smaller nets usually take students more practice to consistently produce "pancakes." This is why I always start off students with an eight-footer. The centrifugal force required to open a seven foot or larger cast net is less than you might think.

Generally, a large heavy net will catch more bait. When opened on top of the same sized bait school, in the same conditions, you can expect more bait to be caught in a larger net. This is why I am usually throwing the largest cast net possible within legal regulations. *One and done!*

However, there are situations where a small net might "out-fish" the bigger nets.

For example, I could be chasing small, fast-moving schools of mullet. The mullet are wise to my every movement. I must throw the net as far as possible to get ahead of them. For this, I'll use a six or eight-foot cast net specially designed for throwing to the end of the rope, maximizing my "reach" ...and stealth.

I'm targeting the patch of water where I think the school will be - not where they are. Just like a quarterback leading a receiver. It's the same thing for leading a school of baitfish.

But every day is different. There are some days when the bait is on the bottom in about fifteen feet of water, and a small net just won't get down to them and the baits can easily escape. Keep in mind that the deeper the water, the more the cast net will collapse before it hits the bottom. We call this "coning". Deep water cast net fishing is probably the toughest challenge, especially with current.

Shallow Water vs. Deep Water

Depending on the season and where you are in the world, baitfish will gather in an array of different habitats. Some days I find big beautiful pilchards up on the flats of Biscayne Bay in less than two feet of water. Talk about a home run! One pancake and I'm on my way to go catch a trophy.

Other days, the pilchards are loitering near the bottom of an inlet 20 feet below the surface with ripping current. These are the days when mother nature and the fishing gods make you work for your live baits.

Regardless of where the baits are found, I'll help you bring the proper tools for the job. Here are a few examples and tactics to deal with them:

➤ **Shallows:** When I am targeting bait in the shallows, I don't need an extra heavy net or even a large net. I prefer my all-purpose eight-foot cast net weighted out to 1.25 lb. per foot. It is heavy enough to get the bait fast but light enough not to take up a ton of grass or sand. I also don't want to damage any grass flats. You could go even lighter, down to about 1 lb. per foot but that is just about as light as I would recommend. It is quite a treat to be able to mug the baits and hardly break a sweat in the shallows.

➤ **Deep Water:** Targeting bait in water deeper than six feet requires the correct cast net along with a sound strategy. First, you need a cast net with the right mesh size. If you are targeting baits longer than five inches, you'll want to use a cast net built with half-inch mesh. Why does the size of the bait matter? It matters because you don't want the baits to escape through mesh that is too big or get "gilled" by a mesh that is just big enough for the baits to poke their heads through but not big enough for the baits to escape. If you wind up with a net full of gilled baits, you'll get to enjoy the next 30 minutes as you work to remove every single gilled bait from your net because you can't use the net again until the gilled baits have been removed.

That being said, if you are targeting bait longer than 8", you can jump up to a 1" mesh. The larger mesh allows the net to sink faster by allowing more water to travel through each mesh square. It's called "physics."

You will also need a heavy net: one that is weighted to 1.5 lb. per foot. Although this makes for a heavy throw, you need the cast net to sink as quickly as possible to surround the school of baits. Again, your strategy is to be "one and done": Catch all of your live baits in one toss and go fishing! I'll bring three nets for use in deep water in varying mesh sizes to cater to the size of the baits I'm targeting. These cast nets are heavy and take quite a bit out of me to open numerous times, especially on a hot and humid summer day. By being patient, I wait for everything to align before making my cast. Maximizing the amount of bait in each throw is key.

One and Done:
Throwing the net once to yield enough bait to go fishing.

How A Cast Net Sinks

Alright. We've determined that heavier nets tend to catch more bait, but are not tailored for every situation. Now, let's look at how a cast net sinks. Learning the physics of how cast nets behave will help you analyze the outcome of each throw and how to adjust.

Weight and mesh size of the cast net affects how your cast net sinks over the targeted bait. Water depth and speed of current also play a part. Keep these conditions in mind when choosing a cast net.

Let's say you are targeting a bait school in ten feet of water, and they are sitting on the bottom. You load up a twelve-foot cast net that is 1.5 pound per foot, which is about twenty pounds of net with the webbing and components.

You open the perfect pancake: a twenty-four-foot diameter "no fly zone" when it hits the water. However, as the net is sinking down to the bottom, it's collapsing. By the time it reaches the bait school, the leads have pulled the net in, reducing your diameter significantly. Still, it offers very good coverage and that's the best we can ask for.

We actually experimented with adding over 1.7 pound per foot to our half-inch mesh cast net. Even though the net sank faster, the opening collapsed much faster, resulting in fewer baits. So, there is a point of diminishing returns when considering the weight of your cast net.

Understanding the physics of cast netting will ultimately aide your decision to choosing the right cast net in order to yield the most amount of bait.

CHAPTER 4
CHOOSING THE RIGHT CAST NET

How to Select the Right Cast Net

Now that you know how a cast net is designed and constructed as well as the physics, it's time to pick out the perfect net FOR YOU.

For high-level bait fishermen, there is no single cast net that is perfect for all scenarios. Do you bring only one fishing rod offshore or only one lure to fish the backcountry? Of course not. The same holds true for cast nets. The best fishermen will carry as many as five cast nets to cover all situations, and sometimes even more. You never know what mother nature will throw at you. Studying the seasons and patterns of baitfish is key to knowing which net you will be working with during a given trip.

For example, during the pilchard spawn off Miami, we get big baits on the bottom in varying depths. My net of choice is a fourteen-foot, half-inch mesh and 1.5 pound per foot net. I call this net "The Hulk." It's big, heavy and designed to sink fast without gilling baits. It's a brute!

I only want to throw the Hulk a few times - hopefully I can load it up on the first toss. Some days, I really must work at it and others are "one-and-done." Tossing the Hulk takes a lot out of me, especially when I'm fishing solo. Driving the boat and using the big cast nets is serious high-level angling, so maximizing each throw is key.

As the spring ends and gives way to summer, the small baits averaging three inches are right off the beaches. It's probably some of the easiest bait fishing there is. They are literally right at your feet in the breaking surf. I use my lightweight five-foot, quarter-inch mesh and 1.25 pound per foot net for these critters. I'm usually on foot, hence traveling light is key. There is no need for a big and heavy cast net to weigh me down when the baits are plentiful. I must cover ground, get bait and find the fish.

And the list goes on and on.

When picking out a cast net, consider the following:

The Three Metrics for Choosing a Net

Remember: There are three (3) metrics to net selection: Size, Mesh, and Weight. Let's explore each of these in greater detail:

➤ **Size**: If you have never thrown a cast net, start with an eight-foot, 3/8 mesh and 1.25lb per foot. It works for most baits between 3" and 12". It is heavy enough to work in deep water and light enough for the shallows. Adults and teenagers can easily learn to throw pancakes with this size, especially using the triple-load method.

➤ Most of you will only need this one cast net. Once you master this net and the triple-load method, you can work your magic with larger or smaller nets to expand your range.

Years ago, I realized it is far easier for students to learn on bigger nets than smaller nets. It's also much more gratifying to throw a perfect circle of sixteen feet, rather than something much smaller. The sheer joy of watching a student fire out a perfect pancake is priceless. I just love being a part of it. Some students learn to toss "pancakes" in as few as ten minutes.

If you're fishing beaches and lakes, you won't need a net much bigger than five feet and 1/4 inch mesh. I use this particular net all summer long to catch pilchards, sardines, croakers and even big mullet.

To sum it up, determine the application for your net. Start with a six or eight-footer and ask yourself, "How much bait do I need to catch?" If you only need a dozen or two dozen baits, then the eight-footer will be your best friend. And once you are throwing "pancakes" with the eight-footer, you can expand your mastery of other net sizes – both larger and smaller.

➤ **Mesh:** Once you determine your desired net size/diameter, you'll need to select a mesh size. If you are looking for an all-purpose mesh size, I say go with 3/8" as it will work for most baits between 3" and 12." I have caught just about everything with a 3/8" mesh and it's the net I throw most of the time. This is the net I will bring with me when I'm fishing on boats other than my own, rather than lugging each one of my nets. This is truly my "Go-To" Net.

If you don't know the size baitfish you are targeting, stick with a 3/8" mesh and adjust accordingly. If the baits are getting "gilled" or stuck in the net, then drop down to ¼" mesh.

The cast net's mesh size also plays a major role in the amount of weight needed and sink rate of the net. Smaller-mesh cast nets such as 3/16" and 1/4", will need more weight to sink as fast as a net with, say, 1/2" mesh. There is no getting around the laws of physics: The water simply can't travel through the small mesh squares fast enough, so the lead line must work harder to pull the webbing down in the water column.

➤ **Weight:** Cast nets are offered in many different weights. Cheap, inferior nets typically weigh in at a ratio of less than one pound per foot. A high-quality, custom performance cast net such as a JuJu is available in 1.25 and 1.5 pound per foot. You want your net to sink as fast as possible! Weight can be the most difficult metric to identify because many net manufacturers don't disclose the true weight of their nets.

Most manufacturers choose to ignore that we *ten percenters* require nets that sink as fast as possible. Using my effortless method of throwing, you need not fear nets being too heavy. We want to catch more bait and go fishing sooner!

Elite cast net fishermen prefer heavy nets, some prefer more than 1.5 pound per foot. So will YOU. That doesn't mean you must go extra heavy; just purchase something of quality. I've found that heavier nets equate to quality construction. I also prefer the spherical, marble-shaped leads as they don't tangle like the rectangular or torpedo-shaped leads. The marble-shaped leads also sink faster. When I see marble-shaped leads, I think high-end net.

If you are throwing on bait schools and find that you are coming up empty despite perfect openings, the culprit may be a net with insufficient weight. We've all been there: You open a perfect pancake right on top of the bait fish and pull up... nothing! It's because you're just not getting on top and trapping them fast enough. The baits have plenty of time to scatter before your net descends to trap them. And even if they get trapped inside, they will wait patiently for you to pull in your net, while they find the spaces between the leads to escape. Mullet are especially clever at this. So, be mindful of the weight of your net. Don't be afraid to buy cast nets of varying weights. We'll come back to this in a bit.

Keep in mind that there are very special situations where a light cast net could be advantageous.

For example, if you are catching bait in shallow water or over a grass flat, the bait really have nowhere to go. Even though I still prefer a heavy cast net, especially when targeting mullet, you can get away with a lighter net. A lighter cast net will not bring in a bunch of grass or sand with it as well, thus preserving the habitat. It's also much easier to throw a net that is a fraction the weight. This comes in handy when the bait fish are not cooperating and you need to throw several times.

Another great application for a light cast net is netting baits on the beach: You won't get worn out carrying a lighter net a half mile down the beach. (Check out some of my YouTube videos to see this strategy in action.)

If you are lucky enough to be catching bait in shallow water, then cherish it. Those are the easy days and as a live bait fisherman, you really learn to appreciate them.

Now that you know the three metrics to cast a net, let's expand on special baits that require special nets.

Specialty Nets: Mullet

There he is - that *ten percenter* guy I keep talking about, and he's crushing the bait... yet again. He's loading up on mullet, cast after cast, while everyone else is pulling up absolutely nothing.

Why is he so good? What's he doing differently than the rest of us?

It's simple. He's using a cast net that is tailor-made for his application. It's specifically designed for one purpose: Netting Mullet. Having the right cast net could be the difference between filling your livewells or coming up empty-handed.

Some days, netting mullet can be effortless. You simply find a school on the surface, their backs out of the water, oblivious to danger and you make that perfect opening, yielding more than enough bait to go fishing. This scenario plays out during or just after the Florida Mullet Run, usually occurring September through November.

However, when the bait schools thin out, you will have to work hard for them - I mean *really* work. There are days when I average only one mullet per hour!

Because nearly everything that swims and flies eats them, mullet spend their entire lives on the run. They are on high alert every second of every day. They are at the bottom of the food chain and the bigger they are, the smarter they are. Any signs of your presence will send them scattering.

It took me nearly twenty years to invest in a cast net specifically designed for mullet. I grew tired of the struggle (and by now you know that I am always looking to improve). I've designed and built the perfect cast net to catch mullet!

As you learned earlier, the key factors in net selection are size, mesh and weight. Let's start with size. Since mullet schools can disperse quickly when your net hits the water, I want a net that is no smaller than six feet.

Now, let's address mesh size. I recommend 5/8" and 1 1/8" mesh. That's right, two different nets depending on the target size mullet. The large mesh squares enable the net to sink quickly over the top of the mullet school. The bigger the mesh, the faster the sink rate, by allowing more water to travel through each square.

Lastly, you will want an extra-heavy net. I designed and built a ten-footer that weighs 1.5 pound per foot. This net sinks like a rock and isn't so heavy that it wears me out. All the better reason to make every cast count. It's plenty big and heavy, yet agile enough for me to get distance. This net is also designed with a double-selvage at the horn and a double leadline to accommodate the increased weight – it's similar to beefing up the suspension of a truck.

When comparing this custom-built mullet net to a standard ten-foot, 3/8" mesh net at 1.25 pounds per foot, the 3/8" cast net will sink too slowly to catch many, or any, mullet - especially in deeper water. That's not to say that the all-purpose, Multi 3/8" cast net cannot get the job done. It's just that the custom mullet cast net is ideally-suited to make the most out of every toss.

For years, I caught all the mullet I needed with a 3/8" mesh net. It wasn't until about ten years ago that I built a true mullet cast net with the features above and this net turned into an absolute game-changer! Now, my mullet sessions usually last about twenty minutes and when I throw on top of mullet, there is no escaping. The net sinks rapidly and the mullet never see it coming.

Minnow Cast Nets

We learned that in order to catch big baits such as mullet and bunker, you need a heavily weighted cast net with large mesh. On the opposite side of the spectrum are some of the smallest baits: Anchovies and Silversides. Yep, those same fish you find on a pizza or a Caesar salad.

These diminutive baits are typically around one inch long and require a specialty cast net. This is the one scenario where your all-purpose eight foot, 3/8" mesh will not work. In fact, it would be a total disaster to throw a 3/8" mesh on top of one-inch baits. The result would be "Christmas in July" with thousands of dead baits stuck in each mesh square. *Ten percenters* know this.

Anchovies are not a hearty bait species and, quite frankly, make better dead baits or chum. Anglers will often freeze large quantities of anchovies due to their high mortality rate. Therefore, the correct cast net is key. A proper minnow cast net consists of 3/16" mesh. This is some of the smallest mesh you will see in a cast net. The smaller mesh squares don't allow the baits to push their head through and get stuck.

Owning multiple cast nets that are tailored to specific species and conditions separates the Pros from the Joes. The *ten percenters* show up to their bait spots with several nets prepared for any situation. Now, you can too.

In the next chapter, I will give you what you really came for.

I will arm you with two methods of throwing your cast net that I have perfected through countless hours of throwing myself and teaching hundreds of students.

Are you ready to start throwing "pancakes"?

CHAPTER 5
HOW TO THROW A CAST NET

Introduction to the Techniques

To load and open a cast net, there are several methods that work and there are many others that do not. I have tried more than I care to admit—from putting the lead line in your teeth to doing crazy spins and falling out of the boat! I have seen all of the shapes and sizes that result: tacos, empanadas, bananas and of, course, pancakes!

Consistency is the key. Can you **consistently** open the cast net into a perfect circle? I'm talking 9 out of 10 times! This is the question you need to ask yourself with the method you currently use. If you cannot consistently open your net in a full circle, then it's time to improve, starting right now.

In this chapter, I will teach you the two methods that I've perfected over the years. You will never have to put the lead line in your mouth again and the motion will be effortless. The method you choose depends on the size and weight of the net. You are welcome to try them both and pick the best one for you. I will alternate between the two methods, depending on the application and conditions.

Before we practice tossing that perfect "pancake," I must warn about the dangers of cast netting and make sure you practice safety. It's my job to prepare you for all aspects of using a cast net and it starts right now with awareness.

Cast Net Safety

I have seen needless accidents over the years, from people falling out of their boats to being pulled in by the handline. These accidents are

PREVENTABLE, as you will see below. I was once told by an attorney that there are no such things as "accidents"; there is only negligence. Let's NOT be negligent.

You never know what mother nature will throw at you such as tides, currents, wind, waves, marine life and lighting conditions. You also have to contend with factors beyond your control such as other boaters, debris, etc.

With this in mind, here's how you can prevent accidents from happening:

When attaching the loop of the handline to your wrist, **do so loosely.** Do NOT affix the loop to your wrist in a strong noose-type knot, whereby the loop gets tighter with more tension on the handline.

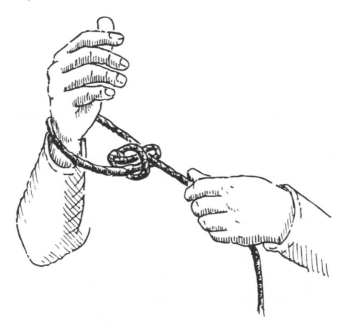

Why the loose loop? If you throw your net from a moving boat and it gets stuck in the propeller, a rock, or on top of a shark, you could very well get pulled in. This scenario has played out countless times. Don't let it happen to you.

Simply attach the handline loosely. If your net gets caught somewhere, the rope will pull right off, rather than pull you in. Most nets have floating line too, so you'll be able to retrieve it. I'd rather you lose your cast net, than something much worse.

When throwing on massive schools of bait, guess what's nearby? Predators! And if you throw enough, you will catch them in your net. One time, I inadvertently netted a hundred-pound spinner shark. Not good! It could have turned into a disaster. Because I had the loop of the handline loosely over my wrist, I wasn't in any danger.

I have also had close calls when chucking big nets in a strong current. If the net gets stuck on the bottom while aboard a boat rapidly drifting with the current, I'm at risk of getting pulled overboard – and FAST. I know mates and professional bait fishermen that keep a dive knife strapped to their leg or hanging on a lanyard, just in case of this very situation.

Please listen and practice safety out there. I've had near accidents myself and witnessed others. I want everyone to have fun while learning, but it's important to mitigate the dangers involved.

Here are some other safety tips to consider while cast netting:

- Do not stand on the gunnel of your boat while throwing your cast net. Remain inside the boat for maximum stability.

- Do not throw your cast net with your boat's motor in gear. Your net could easily get caught in the propeller of the motor. Simply put your motor in neutral when throwing and retrieving your net.

Alright. I've said my piece. No more "running with scissors" warnings.

Now, are you ready to use that cast net of yours? Let's get started.

How To Clear A Cast Net

Before we dive right into the techniques of opening your net in a perfect circle, it is imperative that you learn how to clear your cast net. Clearing a net simply means ridding it of any tangles in the braille lines and lead line. It also means removing any debris or baitfish from previous throws, essentially a perfectly clean net.

No matter how you chose to open your cast net, a tangle or debris will result in a poor throw…and frustration. A professional golfer would never swing a wedge that has dirt in the grooves. They always start with a perfectly clean tool of the trade and you should too.

Remember, paying attention to the finer details is what keeps you a member of the ten percenters. The best fishermen pay close attention to every little step in their mission to catch the most bait with the fewest attempts. The quicker you load up on bait, the sooner you get to go fishing. Also keep in mind that you may only get one shot at the bait school. Make it count!

Now, let's clear that net.

Step 1: Clear the Braille lines

Clearing the braille lines of a cast net is often overlooked by recreational anglers. The more you net bait, the more tangles and twists you will get in your braille lines. The pros check to ensure that their braille lines are perfect before every cast. The Joes just wing it and hope for the best. The pros also clear the braille lines immediately after unloading baits. This prepares them faster for the next throw and allows them to shake out any dead baits or debris that remain in the net.

Use your finger to split the braille lines apart all the way to swivel. Run your finger starting from the bottom going up, clearing any twists you see.

When clearing your net aboard a boat, do so over the gunnel into the water, to give yourself more room and height, in order to place more tension on the braille lines. This will be especially useful with nets 10 feet or larger.

Next, drop the net back down and grab the horn, allowing the braille lines to straighten out to the length of the net perfectly.

Step 2: Clear the Lead Line

Start by whipping the lead line over your leg and running through it with your hand until you come to the end. If you come across a braille line that is under or over the lead line, simply fix it there. You're also removing debris and bait from previous throws during this process. Even the smallest piece of seaweed is enough to hang up a net. With lower-quality nets that utilize rectangular or torpedo-shaped leads, the leads often get entangled in the braille lines. This is why I prefer cast nets with marble-shaped leads that won't tangle nearly as much.

You want your net to be in this tangle-free condition each and every time before loading. Only when your net is completely twist-free and clear of tangles can you open perfect pancakes.

Clearing a net should become part of your cast net ritual, each and every time you load up. You should get to the point that you subconsciously clear the net without even thinking about it. It's such a ritual for me that I'm looking for baits while I'm clearing the net...by feel. Even while I'm reloading, I'm looking for the next school to target.

Now that you have a clear cast net, it's time to load it.

Now You're Ready!

Following are the two different methods I have perfected and use on a daily basis to fill my livewells with fresh live bait.

The first method you will learn I call the "No-Teeth Technique".

Introduction to the "No-Teeth Technique"

Remember when I told the story of how my buddy taught me the most amazing method to open my ten-foot cast net? Well, that's coming soon. But there was a problem: The method didn't help me with cast nets smaller than eight feet. Plus, I was getting soaked! I needed to learn a new way of opening smaller nets to target mullet and other baitfish in shallow water.

Growing up in Miami, I watched Cuban fishermen toss their nets daily. It was like being at a concert and watching the drummer up close. I couldn't take my eyes off of them.

They consistently produced perfect "pancakes" and they projected their nets far—all while staying dry and clean.

Those Cuban fishermen used six-foot to ten-foot nets and I never saw them load their nets by placing the lead line in their teeth nor over their shoulders. I paid close attention and studied their method. Soon I got it (or a variation of it) and I could open my smaller cast nets easily and quickly. Best of all, I stayed dry and clean! This came in handy for some fishing adventures before school.

And now, I would now like to introduce to you the "No-Teeth Method." This will be perfect for nets from five feet up to eight feet. You won't get dirty or wet and you'll be able to rocket the net all the way out to the end of your handline to reach those timid baits. You'll also be able to use this method to reload quickly after a cast to make a "snap cast."

Let's get started.

No-Teeth Method (5ft to 8ft Cast Nets)

Step 1. ALWAYS Clear Your Cast Net

To get your net fully open, you must clear your net of any twists, tangles and debris. Run your hands throughout the net to ensure there are no leads caught on the braille lines. Remove any debris or previously caught baitfish stuck in the net.

Step 2: Attach Handline to Wrist

Place the loop of the handline around the wrist of your strong arm. I'm a righty, therefore, I use my right wrist. If you're a lefty, do the opposite throughout this instruction.

DO NOT secure the handline to your wrist in such a way that you can't get it off of your wrist-**QUICKLY**-if an emergency occurs.

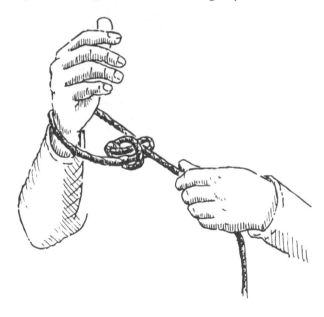

Step 3: Coil the Handline

Make one to two-foot coils with the handline until you reach the horn of your cast net. Pull the horn to the top of your coils, allowing the braille lines to run all the way through the net.

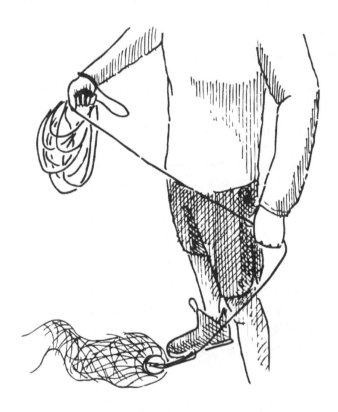

No-Teeth Method (5ft to 8ft Cast Nets)

Step 1. ALWAYS Clear Your Cast Net

To get your net fully open, you must clear your net of any twists, tangles and debris. Run your hands throughout the net to ensure there are no leads caught on the braille lines. Remove any debris or previously caught baitfish stuck in the net.

Step 2: Attach Handline to Wrist

Place the loop of the handline around the wrist of your strong arm. I'm a righty, therefore, I use my right wrist. If you're a lefty, do the opposite throughout this instruction.

DO NOT secure the handline to your wrist in such a way that you can't get it off of your wrist-QUICKLY-if an emergency occurs.

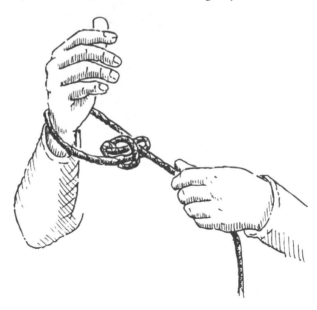

Step 3: Coil the Handline

Make one to two-foot coils with the handline until you reach the horn of your cast net. Pull the horn to the top of your coils, allowing the braille lines to run all the way through the net.

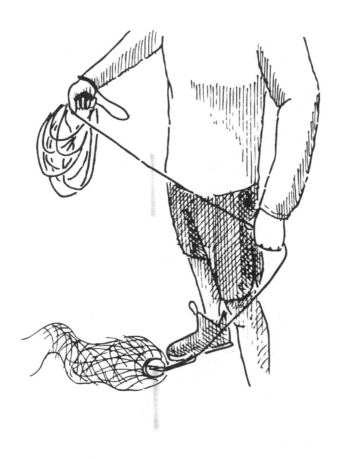

Before you take your first grab, take one last look at the net to ensure it is clear of twist. If the net is twisted before you grab it, the net will not fully open, reducing your diameter.

Step 4: The First Load

Depending on the size of the net, grab it about one to two feet below the horn. You do not need to grab your net at the horn (this is a common mistake). By grabbing the net about a foot or two under the horn, it is more manageable to your height, making it much easier to throw. This also reduces wear and tear on the horn itself.

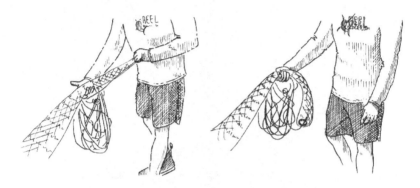

Step 5: Split the Net

Split the net into two equal sections, or "piles", and stand between each pile, all while maintaining your initial grab from Step 4.

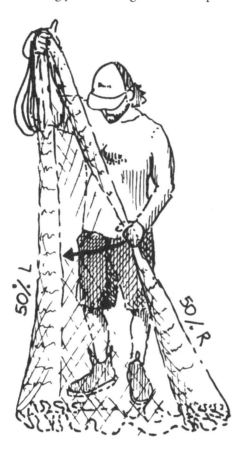

Step 6: The Second Load

Run your left hand down the net to about waist-high. Make your second grab just below your waist using your right hand. If you want to throw the net further, then grab the net further down, closer to your knee. (You'll be able to experiment with what works best by practicing with different grabs.) Do this step while keeping the net split into two piles, with the leads on the ground.

MIDDLE

The entire net should be in your right hand (or dominant hand).

Step 7: Rotate Lead Piles

This is the key Step and the step that proves challenging to many of my students: Grab the lead pile on your left side about halfway down to the lead line and flip it over your right hand. You'll notice you have two staggered levels to your lead piles when done correctly.

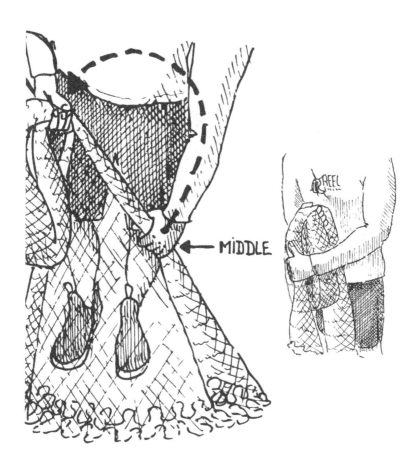

Step 8: First Lead Line Grab

With your right hand, grab the lead line that joins the two levels.

Place the lead line on the top of your right hand and hold in place by sticking your thumb up.

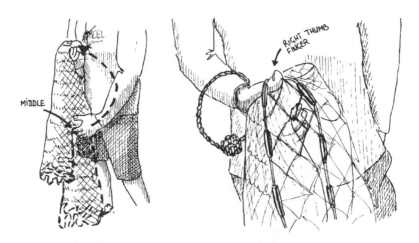

Step 9: Second Lead Line Grab

Reach down to the lead line directly off your thumb and grab it with your left hand (this is the last piece to go when you throw).

Step 10: Cast the Net

Create initial momentum by rocking the net slightly behind you and then out in front of you. Use a smooth motion and don't get carried away. Remember: Less is more.

Turn your right hand over during the throw while holding the lead line in your left hand a second or two longer. This move is similar to finishing a golf swing.

In the illustration below, notice that my left hand is still holding the lead line-for a split second-while the cast net is in the air. This is key to getting the net to open in a full circle, a pancake.

The "No-Teeth Method" works great for nets between the sizes of five and eight feet. As you get into the bigger and heavier nets, it will take a lot of strength to fire off the net using this technique. For this reason, I will teach you a method that is effortless and allows the weight of the leads to do the work for you.

We call it the "Triple-Load" method. Let's jump right in and learn it!

Triple-Load Technique

(8ft to 14ft Cast Nets / Heavy Cast Nets)

When teaching seminars, it became apparent to me that the following technique is the easiest for all levels of athletic ability. You don't need to be strong or tall to open up the largest of cast nets.

By learning the "triple-load method", my students could throw perfect circles right away. And by watching them closely, I refined my teaching method to the point that you will pick up this method quickly and confidently. I can almost recall every student as they threw a perfect pancake for the first time. It was pure joy to witness.

Unlike the "no teeth" method, the triple-load method requires very little strength. You will use the centrifugal force of the leads to coax the net wide open.

The objective is to divide the net into three "pieces" or "loads" to distribute the weight amidst your body—about a third over your shoulder and a third in each hand.

This method leads to a nearly effortless throw with an eight or ten-foot cast net. And as you get into the heavy nets such as twelve and fourteen-footers, it's the same technique. You just need a few small tweaks.

I equate the Triple Load method to throwing a frisbee or swinging a golf club. Just like a golfer loads the swing into his left side, the same is done with the triple-load technique. Throwing large and heavy cast nets is done with your lower body, not so much your arms. Strength is not as important as rhythm.

So, if you can throw a frisbee or swing a golf club, you can fully open a large and heavy cast net. Guaranteed.

**Pro Tip:** Practice throwing a heavy medicine ball to a friend to get a feel for the technique. You won't be able to throw it with your arms. You'll need to turn your body back, and then use your lower body to fire it forward.

Note: You <u>will</u> get wet! Unless you can be one and done, this method will not be as clean as the "No Teeth" technique. However, when you have a livewell full of fresh baits, you won't care. Just bring a spare shirt.

Now, let's get started. Follow these steps to take advantage of the Triple-Load Method:

Step 1: Clear the Net

Clear your cast net of any twist or tangles in the braille lines and lead line.

Step 2: Attach Handline to Wrist

Place the loop of the handline around the wrist of your OPPOSITE dominant hand. I'm a righty. Therefore, I use my left wrist. If you're a lefty, do the opposite throughout this instruction.

Step 3: Coil Handline

Coil the handline in two-foot coils around your strong opposite hand. I hold the coils in my left hand since I am right-handed. Since I throw a frisbee off my right side, I like to throw my net from the same side of my body.

Check one more time to ensure your net is clear.

4: The First Load

Make your first grab under the horn about two to three feet down the net. Avoid the common mistake of grabbing at the horn. On an eight-foot net, I grab about 2 feet from the horn and on a twelve-foot net, about 3 feet.

__Tip:__ Make your first grab by placing the webbing of the net between your fingers. This will free up much needed space in your palm for the rest of the load. Some cast nets fit all in one hand. However, many nets on the market are thick and will not easily fit in your palm without large hands.

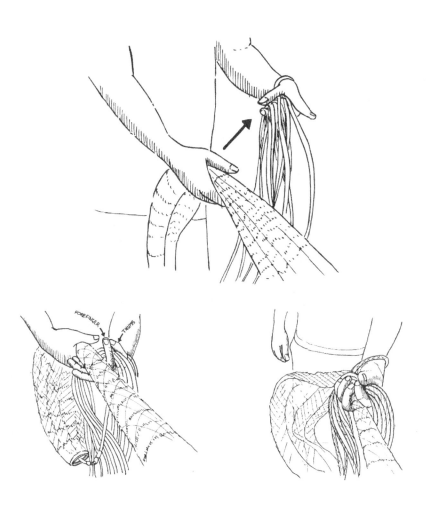

Step 5: The Second and Third Load

Make your second grab about waist high using your right hand. If you are loading a twelve or fourteen-footer, your second grab will be about three feet down from the first and then you'll take a third grab waist-high.

Step 6: Separate a Third

On the right side of the net, separate about a third of it. You'll want to play with the amount here, depending on the size net you are throwing.

Step 7: Place First Load Over Shoulder

With about 1/3 of the net, go around your left elbow and up and over your left shoulder.

Rest the leads over your shoulder and down your back. The weight of the net in your hand should be pulling down and to your front to keep the net securely over your shoulder in position.

Step 8. Divide the Rest of the Net

Grab the inside lead line with your right hand and divide the rest of the net in half using a fanning motion. Take the half you just created and drop it over your right leg keeping it separated from the rest of the net.

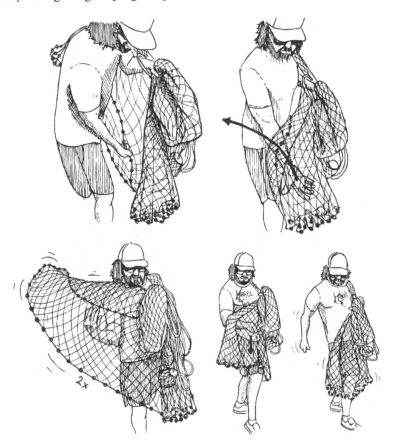

Step 9: Grab the Last Third of Net

With your right pinky finger, grab the lead line between your left hand and over your leg. Then grab the right side of the net with your right hand. You want your hands only about a foot apart to reduce the power needed to throw a heavy net.

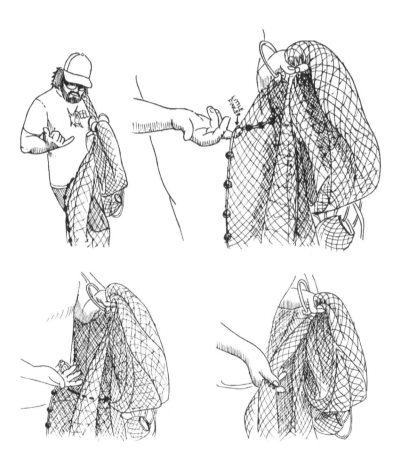

Step 10: Cast the Net

To cast the net, push it off your body and let the leads swing back and behind you while utilizing a full shoulder turn. Do so with finesse and a steady motion. You want the leads to work for you, in a pendulum-like motion.

As the leads reach their highest point behind you, bring the net forward as if you are swinging a bucket full of water and, at the top of your arc, let the leads fall naturally and explode out in a frisbee like motion. This allows the gravity of the weights to move the net away from you as it opens.

The last piece of net to leave your hands will be in your right pinky. Don't worry about holding it too long, as the momentum will pull it out of your hand naturally. This should only take a split second.

Close the net full of bait and go catch some fish!

As you're practicing, I want you to start with short, fluid motions. Don't allow the net to swing too far back behind you. You'll find the less you try, the easier it is to open into a full circle. Many of my students over-compensate and try to muscle the net open. This is a huge mistake. As they practice, I'll caution them, "Do less, do less"! I will even ask them to throw the net in slow motion and yet they still throw too hard.

Pro Tip: *Bring an extra shirt to change in to after "making bait". You will get wet with the Triple Load method, but your live wells will be jam-packed! I usually change into a dry shirt after loading the livewells. I feel like a new person, instantly rejuvenated!*

How to Fix Your Mistakes (Triple Load Method)

It happens to the best of us. After a cast gone wrong, you will hear me mumble in frustration, "Dangit! I didn't get all of it."

I knew before the net hit the water that I had made a mistake that cost me bait. Sometimes I'll know it even as the net is leaving my hands. This really irks me, but it happens to all of us – even *ten percenters.*

When you throw a perfect "pancake," you should get that "notched-in" feeling that it will be a good one. Just as when a golfer strikes the sweet spot of the club face, does a twirl and watches the ball fly through the air, you can just *feel* it. And that feeling gets cemented in your brain. As soon as the net gets air, you'll *know* whether the result will be a perfect pancake or a taco!

It used to shock me to see professional charter captains throw less than perfect circles – sometimes brutal taco-shaped tosses. But now, I know it happens to even the best of us. The cause could be as minor as a small stick or piece of seaweed stuck in the net, not allowing the net to fully open.

Sometimes, the culprit is simply user error or fatigue. (Sigh) It happens. Nobody makes a perfect cast each and every time, not even me. After all, Steph Curry doesn't make all of his free-throws either. We're human and mistakes will happen out there. What sets us apart from the 90 percenters is that we decide to learn from our mistakes in our quest to open the net perfectly every, single time.

The great thing about learning to throw a cast net is that you receive instant feedback. The net doesn't lie: If the net isn't a perfect circle, then you've done something wrong.

Don't sweat it. Learn from your mistakes. Here's how you can fix it:

Make a practice cast on an open piece of grass. (Make sure there is plenty of room to accommodate your fully-opened cast net.) Once you've cast your net on the grass, analyze the opened net as four quadrants. This is how you can determine which part of your load you'll need to adjust.

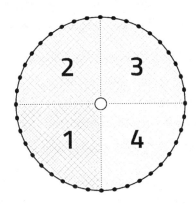

Quadrant 1: If you've opened your net but the first quadrant is closed, you put too much net over your shoulder. Re-load and, this time, use 1/3 or less over your shoulder. Experiment until you get the amount just right. Most of my students usually put too much over their shoulder when starting out, resulting in this quadrant closed during the throw.

Quadrant 2: If you've opened your net but the upper left is not fully opened, then you must adjust the amount of net loaded in your left hand. You most likely have more than a third of the net in your left hand or you didn't clear the net of tangles or debris. Pay close attention when you split the net in half to ensure that you truly have fifty percent of the remainder in each hand.

Quadrant 3: If you've opened your net but it looks like the shape of a taco on the right side, then you must adjust what's happening in your right hand. Either you split the net with too much into your right hand, or you're holding on to it too long. Adjust and try again.

Quadrant 4: This is the piece that is in your pinky. If it is not laying right, then you most likely need to hold the lead line in your pinky finger a bit longer or shorter. Once you get it right, it will become natural. Reload and try again.

Practice, Practice, Practice

There are very few anglers who can simply pick up a cast net and cast it as though they were born to throw perfect pancakes. As with any other sports and pursuits, mastery takes hours of practice, self-evaluation and a constant striving to improve.

Commercial live bait guys are masters because they use their cast nets EVERY SINGLE DAY.

Their technique is not even a concern anymore – it's second nature for them. Just like professional golfers who play for low scores, a live bait fisherman wants to throw the net as few times as possible and yield as much bait as possible.

Recreational anglers will throw cast nets as many as 10 times more than a pro. Why? The pro always waits for the perfect time to strike.

I recommend that you practice your cast net openings on a large grassy area so as not to damage the net or the leadline. Throwing your cast net over concrete and hard surfaces might chafe and deform your lead lines or otherwise damage the net.

Also, make an effort to record yourself with your phone or video camera to evaluate your loading, casting and retrieval methods. Once you can effortlessly open that perfect circle on the lawn over and over, you'll have the confidence to hit the water and do it for real. I recommend that you move your practice sessions to the water. I can't tell you how many people I know who can fire off pancakes on the lawn but, when I put them on a boat, they throw a restaurant full of tacos!

When netting baits from a rocking and rolling boat, you must account for current, wind, obstacles, moving baitfish, etc. Extend your practice regimen to netting actual bait schools from the boat. You don't even need to fish. Just empty the net at boatside when you bring it in. Devote an entire day to catching bait and mastering your cast net in shallow water, deep water, off beaches, lakes, near oyster bars, etc.! You can also treat your practice as your cardio workout! We don't call it sport fishing for nothing! There should be nothing relaxing about catching bait.

CHAPTER 6
THE ART OF CAST NETTING

How to Close A Cast Net

OK. Now that you've opened your cast net into a perfect "pancake," your work is not done, hence the "art of cast netting" begins! So many people spend a lot of effort learning how to fully open a cast net, but they don't spend time learning how to properly close the net.

The best cast net fishermen share this trait in common: they use their cast net to form a bag to enclose the baits before bringing them into the boat. The pros are nonchalant when bringing up the net. They can afford to be. They know the baits are trapped and not going anywhere.

Recreational anglers are often the opposite! They panic and rush, as if the baits are magically going to escape this bag, pulling in their handline like madmen.

I get it. I've been there too.

Once you've opened your net over a school of bait, your first instinct is to pull in the net aggressively and retrieve it as fast as possible. However, this is counter-productive and may actually allow some baits to escape. This action may also harm or scale your frisky baits in the process.

Remember what I told you: Once inside your cast net, mullet are waiting for you to pull up, so that they can dart between the gaps between the leads to escape. Well, let's outsmart them. Shall we?

Once you've loaded up on baits, hopefully with a single cast, here is how you should close the net:

➤ Short Tugs: Start by making short tugs of the braille lines. Do not pull in the handline quickly or with long pulls. Not yet. This will close the net the way it was designed to be closed and start forming a bag. This will eliminate the baits' chances to escape between the leads, especially in shallow water, where the net is lying on the bottom.

➤ Slow Pulls: Now, pull up the handline slowly. S-L-O-W-L-Y. There is no rush here. The pros pull slowly because they are treating the baits as gently as possible so that they can live a long time, remain frisky and have the best resale value. You must do the same.

➤ Grab the Horn: Once up to your horn, grab it and bring it up about halfway while holding the handline tight, keeping the net closed. Shake the baits stuck at the top of your net, down and into the formed bag.

➤ Take a Wrap at the Lead Line: Don't bring the net aboard your boat or up onto the seawall using the handline. Instead, take a wrap of the net down close to the lead line. This will take the pressure of your heavy load off the braille lines and make it easier to bring your net into the boat.

If you have a large amount of bait, you can use your elbow to get leverage and lift up with your lower body to bring the net up and into your boat. Now, you can pull up on your horn and release the baits.

Pro Tip: When bringing the net up from deep water on your boat, it is best to go downwind so the net stays away from you and doesn't go under the boat. Simply reposition your boat downwind before pulling up for better results.

How To Transfer Baits Into Your Livewell

You've done it! You've MADE BAIT! Welcome to the *10% club!* And now that you can make bait, the fishing should be a piece of cake!

But there's one more thing I must teach you before you dump those beautiful baits into your livewell: Treat your baits right!

It may seem like I'm nitpicking here, but do you remember when I said the little things in fishing make a big difference? The biggest problem I see with recreational anglers is that they will shove the entire net and lead line right to the bottom of the livewell or bucket before pulling up on the horn. They will then pull the horn and release the baits, with nowhere for the baits to swim freely.

Well, that can work for Joes but not for Pros. Let's do better. Much Better.

When opening up your cast net over your livewell/bucket opening, prevent the lead line from hitting the bottom of your livewell to allow the baits to freely enter the water with no obstruction or any additional trauma. Simply pull up on the horn and dump that fresh bag right into the well. When the baits hit the circulating water inside the livewell, they are free to swim and not bump into any leads or webbing of the net.

And while this is a very small detail, it's a pro move. Keeping baits in the healthiest condition possible should always be your focus. Remember, you just removed the baits from their natural habitat to confine them to a small space. So, let's not stress out the baits any more than we already have.

When the time comes to put those frisky live baits on a hook, you will know exactly what I'm talking about. And that can be the difference between catching fish and getting shut out.

If you are lucky enough to have a boat with a big, in-deck livewell, you have it easy! One of my favorite boats is the Conch 27'. It is configured with huge, spacious livewells in the deck, making it super easy to unload your cast net without any obstruction. I had my latest boat designed specifically for cast netting with an in-deck livewell of sixty gallons for that very reason.

For those of you not blessed with in-deck live wells, don't worry. I've got you covered: Find yourself a laundry bin or fish basket and keep it on the boat. Dump your baits directly into this bin and then carefully pour those baits into your well. I have been doing this for years and it works great! This bin has a massive opening, making it easier to dump the baits into with no obstructions. The bin is also pliable enough that you can keep baits from making "freedom leaps" as you move them to the livewell, unlike buckets.

The better you treat your baits, the healthier they will be when it's time to fish. The best fishermen in the world go above and beyond the call of duty when handling freshly caught live baits – almost to the point of being fanatical. This can be the difference between catching fish or not. A predator cannot resist the natural presentation of a frisky bait, but they may just pass up one that is missing scales or has a case of the "red eye" or "red belly."

When to Cast: Patience Pays

The difference between the Pros and the Joes is that that Pros embrace the power of patience. The Pros seem to move in slow motion. For every ten attempts the Joes make, the Pros require only one or two shots and they're on their way to the fishing grounds. The Pros are confident in their skills to the point of being nonchalant. With a bit of patience, you can emulate the Pros.

Much of the success of cast netting depends on what you do before you even load up the cast net. Plenty of pieces need to fall into place, such as: Determining the baits to target, Locating the baits, Movement of the baits, Water depth, Speed and direction of the wind and current, etc. These pieces will come together to drive your cast net selection and your approach.

Once you've loaded up your net and decided upon your approach, take a few moments to survey the location and the behavior of the baits. In other words, be patient. Don't be in too much of a rush to launch your cast net. At the risk of sounding like a broken record, I cannot stress enough the fact that you may only get one shot at baits in front of you. Make it count by being deliberate and measured.

There have been times when I've loaded up my net but held off casting for as many as thirty minutes until I had the optimum moment to let it fly. I'll watch the sonar to see how deep the water is, how fast the bait is traveling, and which direction. And once I am confident in my strategy, I'll go upwind to ensure I have an easy downwind throw on the bait.

Do you recall the cliché "You only get one chance to make a first impression"? This holds true for that first cast on a school of baits. After your first cast, the baits know you're there and the baits become increasingly more difficult to catch with each toss. Practice patience before your first cast and you will be rewarded.

Slow Down and Load Right

Often, we rush or panic to load the cast net as fast as possible, especially when first spotting a school of bait. Hunters call this panic "buck fever" when hunters rush the shot out of excitement. Pelicans are diving all around the boat, or you see a giant school of bait go airborne as they escape from predators. Of course, you want to launch your net immediately, and as you know by now, the bait school can be gone in the blink of an eye!

Like anything else, if you rush something, you could miss something. In panic mode, you may not clear the net completely or load properly. This could result in a partially-closed cast net when it hits the water, yielding far less bait – or none at all. We call these "tacos"! "Tacos" are the bane of cast netting. This means you will have to toss again and again.

That's the difference between the Pros and the Joes. Pros are calm, collected and deliberate, calculating each move, with one eye on the bait at all times. The Pros are like snipers who wait for that perfect opportunity to attack, all while using far less energy. Sometimes you'll see a Pro work an area without throwing a net for what seems like an eternity, but they are patiently waiting, stalking. Pros would rather open the net once to capture one-hundred baits than cast ten times to catch the same amount.

So, calm down. Take a deep breath. Get in "the zone." Get your net ready in all aspects. You've got this. Take your time and load the net perfectly, while keeping your eye on the bait. Your ability to multi-task at this moment will pay dividends.

Clear any tangles and go through the steps I've taught you. Be methodical and practice a routine that can be repeated in your sleep. Once you hone your technique, your load time will naturally speed up.

Not to brag, but I can load a fourteen-foot net in less than thirty seconds. It is through hundreds of hours of practice and catching bait that this routine has become second nature to me. I load my net without even thinking about the technique.

As I load the net, my mind is focused on the following conditions: Are the baits up top? Are they down deep? Which direction are they moving? Where is the backside of the school? Are they boxed in with only one way to escape? What's the current doing? What's the wind doing?

Treat each cast as if it is your only shot. With a properly-sized cast net and technique to match, you should only NEED one shot. Remember, you may only get one shot at the bait school, so you had better make it count.

Remind yourself to slow down. While you may feel as if you are going in slow motion, trust me. It is to your benefit to relax, load properly and make calculated casts.

Be Confident

I can't stress enough that the success of your cast netting takes place before you slip the handline over your wrist. Do you ever wonder why the truly great ones "make it look easy"? Do you really think that Tiger Woods, Tom Brady, Michael Jordan or Renaldo just roll out of bed and perform at an elite level? Of course not. All the "great ones" practice their craft incessantly, never settling for being "good enough."

A by-product of continually honing your craft is self-confidence – the knowledge that "I've got this!" Professional gamblers have a motto: *Nervous Money Never Wins*. Mastering your cast net includes mastering the mental aspect of your performance.

I want you to practice your casting to the point that you have NO DOUBT that you are going to drop a "pancake" right where you intended, load the livewell with one shot and go fishing!

Stealth: Become a Net Ninja

Do you remember when I said that the *ten percenters* pay close attention to the small details? Netting live bait is no exception. Baitfish may be small, but they are not dumb, especially those full-grown juicy baits you seek.

Baitfish spend their entire lives evading predators from above and below. It cannot be much fun to be a baitfish: they're in the lower echelon of the food chain and their survival depends upon sensing threats as early as possible to make their escape. Their survival instinct also leads baitfish to seek safety in numbers in the form of large schools. As live bait anglers, we can use this behavior to our advantage to load the livewell with just a few throws - or just one. However, that school of bait is still on alert for any threats. You must sneak up on this school to maximize your cast.

From a boat, you are stalking bait in a manner similar to a gamefish or bird. Do you think that predators fill their stomachs by making a racket? Of course not. Predators make their approach as silently as possible to catch the bait school "napping." You need to do this too. You need to be stealthy. You need to become a Net Ninja.

Ninjas were legendary covert agents in 15th century Japan who were respected and feared for their use of stealth to surprise their opponents to strike quickly and disappear. I want you to become a Net Ninja: Using stealth to stalk your target baits, then striking quickly before the school knows what hit it. This means quiet. This means tiptoeing around your gunnels. This means no slamming hatches. This means no music or even conversation with anyone else on board beyond a whisper. This means no slamming your leadline on the deck to clear your net. There is no avoiding physics: Sound travels five times faster in water than it does in the air. If you're not stealthy, your cast net is missing the baits before it ever leaves your hand.

To maintain stealth aboard your boat, eliminate any machinery noises like noisy bilge pumps.

Turn off any electronics that aren't necessary. Trolling motors are stealthy in their own right but be sure to disable the notification "beeps" that indicate things such as speed changes or on/off.

You need to be just as stealthy when netting from land. Those baitfish near the banks or mangroves can feel the vibrations and hear the grass as you step on it. They can also see your silhouette or notice shadows that you may be casting onto the water. The most minute changes to their environment are enough to send them scattering, making your job that much more difficult.

Be stealthy. Become a Net Ninja. Every little trick will help you pack your net with the freshest live baits and most likely on the first throw.

The Unfair Advantage: How to Get Distance with Your Cast Net

Extending the distance with your cast net may be the difference in making bait or not. Extra distance is such an unfair advantage that it's almost cheating. The odds are stacked greatly in your favor when you are a master of launching your net to the end of the handline.

The farther you are from the bait school, the more likely that the baits will never see it coming. If you are working shorelines or beaches, it is a must-have tool in your bag. I can't tell you how many times the baits have been just out of reach of a typical cast and I needed to launch the net some twenty-five feet away. Even when in the boat, spooky baits such as ballyhoo and mullet tend to stay just out of range of the Joes. But the Pros are able to reach out and "touch" them.

And YOU can do it too. You just need to make some small tweaks to the methods that I've just taught you.

It stands to reason that using smaller nets will make it easier for you to cast your net to the length of your handline, especially if you are opening your net from shore. I prefer a net that is eight feet or smaller for gaining as much distance as possible while still taking advantage of sufficient diameter when the net lands atop the school of bait. Even if the net doesn't fully open, it won't matter. The baits never see it coming.

So, here's how we do it:

First, change where you normally grip the net by sliding down closer to your knee, rather than your waist. This will shorten up the net, making it more manageable. Play with this until you find YOUR sweet spot. It will vary based on your height. Then, practice your new load method on a grassy area. Start with a target at about ten feet away and aim for it. I usually use a leaf or a sandal when teaching students. The key is to always have a target!

Allow the gravity of the leads and momentum to work for you. Once you are opening perfect "pancakes" with the horn landing over your target, increase the distance to fifteen feet. And then to twenty, steadily extending your casts to the end of your rope, all while keeping the finesse in your technique. These drills will hone you your abilities and, once you master these distances, you will become a cast net sniper and take your place among the top of the *ten percenters*.

A long-range cast could be your best – and only - opportunity at catching bait. Remember: you want to cast the fewest times possible so that you can get on the bite.

The ability to sneak up on a school and reach it from an extended distance is a skillset that few anglers have mastered. You'll find this skill especially useful when targeting mullet schools that are especially nervous. It may surprise you to find that I have fished with anglers who can fully open fourteen-foot cast nets with no problem yet struggle to consistently launch a "pancake" at long range with a six-foot net.

Once you can launch your net to the end of the handline, you'll join the select few who can make it happen when getting baits is tough. I've armed you with two methods that are great for getting distance. However, you will need to practice and really hone this skill. And when you do, it's game on.

How to Wade with a Cast Net

Some of the most effective bait fishing can be done in shallow water along the banks of lakes, shorelines of beaches and backcountry creeks. These are areas where boats may not be allowed or simply too shallow for boats to access. Baitfish take refuge from predators in shallow water where the big fish can't get to them. They feel safe and have plenty of food. This is why baits congregate near the mangroves, grass flats, etc. Finding a school that is at ease and not moving around is the Holy Grail for live bait anglers.

Small nets are more effective and manageable than large nets when wading. Just like the method you learned previously to launch your net to get distance, the key to getting a good opening is to grip down on the net closer to your knee, allowing you to hold the net up and out of the water. You'll also want to load the cast net before getting in the water to be as stealthy as possible. You do not want the leads to drag in the water as you stalk a school of bait.

Sounds are amplified underwater and any sign of your presence may send the baits scattering. You may only get one chance at bait that has been sitting unmolested all day, so don't blow it by being overzealous. Stalk your prey and make your throw when the timing is perfect. Again, have patience.

This is a high-level technique, and even the best anglers can struggle with it.

Have you ever watched birds such as egrets and herons as they stand in one spot for over an hour before they make a single swipe at a baitfish? I treat my wading sessions as adventures. Although I want to get in and out of there, I will stalk the bait and wait for that perfect opportunity. Too often I have thrown too soon but never too late. Patience is key in the art of cast netting.

Netting from a Bridge or Pier

As a kid, I enjoyed fishing from land. After school, I would fish the lakes of golf courses and on weekends, the local piers. Today, I still love to get out and catch fish with my feet on dry land. There is something about hooking a big fish from land that is double the excitement than that of a boat. And guess what? It all starts with live bait!

When fishing from local bridges and piers, you'll be able to see baitfish and predators from an aerial view, as bait schools congregate right underneath them. Opening a cast net from a bridge or pier can be challenging, especially if you don't have the right cast net - and most anglers don't. Forget about trying your cheap, lightweight cast net from an elevated structure. That net just won't sink fast enough, and the bait will see it coming from a mile away. Typically, when throwing from bridges or piers, you need to make the most out of every shot.

In my experience, I have found the best net to use from a bridge or pier to be an eight-foot, 3/8 mesh at 1.25lb per foot as perfected by the "Multi" series of JuJu Cast Nets. Using my "no-teeth method," I grab down on the net much lower around my knee because I'm usually propelling the net up and over a railing before it goes down to the water.

Opening the net to its full diameter is key here because the lead line will start closing the net as it falls through the air. The greater the distance to the water, the more the net will try to close before hitting the water. Be sure to splice additional line to your handline to ensure that the cast net gets down to the water and sinks over the bait without running out of handline.

As always, practice this method and have patience.

Closing the Net from a Bridge or Pier

When you make a great opening from an elevated structure, let's say higher than ten feet up, you will have a challenge in getting the bait up to you. Let me explain:

If I've just netted a small school of a few dozen baits, I will just pull up the handline immediately and put the baits in my bucket. It is totally acceptable if a few baits get out on the way up. Using those short tugs I told you about will help, especially on mullet, but generally get them up and let's go fishing.

However, if the bait is thick—I'm talking a huge black cloud of bait—I will not throw the net fully open. I will purposely try to throw a taco in efforts of not catching too much bait. Otherwise, I run the risk of popping a braille line or tearing the net on the way back up.

I have had days fishing from piers and bridges where I netted too much bait in the net and snapped the braille lines while trying to pull up my massive haul. Be careful what you wish for. Remember: Most of the time, I'm using a bucket to hold my bait – not a livewell in my boat. I don't NEED a million baits. A three-foot kid's net would have worked just fine in this case.

So, before you throw your cast net off a bridge, consider how thick the bait school is, any underwater structure, current, tide, wind, etc. Note which way the net will drift when it hits the water. You want your net to drift away from the structure, not under it where you could snag pilings or rocks.

Pro Tip: Most of the time, shallow water baits — especially mullet - are focused upward, watching for birds and can see you. Be stealthy, ninja-like. Hide behind pilings. Don't wear bright colored shirts. I will even wear white or ice blue shirts to blend in with the sky.

Cast Netting in Rocky Areas

Baitfish love to congregate in areas of debris, rocks and structure. They didn't survive this long by being stupid. These baits have a knack for hanging over structure that is made to consume cast nets. You'll notice that smaller baits are often easier to capture than larger baits as they just sit there and, at times, even swim into the net. However, those big juicy baits that catch big fish are just the opposite. They're the survivors. Darwinism in action. They spend their entire lives hiding from game fish and pelicans, ospreys and now, YOU. These bait fish can sense threats below and above at all times. So, you need to go ninja mode again, be stealthy!

Here's an example: I have this awesome bait spot in a canal behind a Walmart. Somehow the shopping carts make their way into the water and form an urban small artificial reef. The baitfish love to congregate around the carts as they know they are safe from predators…and my cast net! The carts accumulate algae which mullet love to eat. However, it also houses barnacles, making it a nightmare for cast nets.

At this spot, the only way for me to get the bait is to be patient. I must wait for them to slip up just a bit and meander away from the structure. Risky but effective! I'm not always going to get it right but, by being patient, I can get in and out without shredding up my cast net. Keep in mind that there have been times when the shopping carts won.

As an aside, you had better get good at repairing your cast nets if you are constantly throwing in areas of rocks or structure. While I don't prefer cheap cast nets (after all this is a Mastery Course) you can treat these as "disposable" nets. And while the cheap nets aren't ideal, they just might be all you need to avoid sinking like a rock into a rock.

The key move to catching baits without snagging your net on the subsurface structure is to retrieve the net as soon as it hits the water. If you use a net that is too heavy or let it sink too deep, you will catch a rock, oyster bed or shopping cart that will surely rip your net to shreds. So, keep your handline short and as soon as the net hits the water and has baits, pull it up ASAP. This is the one time that I don't want you to be deliberate or steady. Move quickly to retrieve that net.

If your net does get snagged, DO NOT pull on it aggressively. You will just pop the braille lines and destroy the webbing of the net. If the water is shallow enough, try to get down in the water or use the tip of a fishing rod to release the lead line from the backside. Pulling straight up on the net rather than at an angle will also help. Regardless of whether you can save the cast net, DO NOT leave the net in the water as it will destroy the habitat and continually kill many fish.

5 Cast Netting Mistakes to Avoid

1. DO NOT THROW INTO THE WIND - No matter how strong you are, attempting to open a cast net into the wind is not ideal. Make your way upwind and throw downwind. The net will open effortlessly. Now there are days from the beach, piers and boat where getting upwind is just not an option. In these situations, try to get diagonal to the wind – anything is better than casting squarely into the teeth of the wind. Also, keep your cast low to hopefully cheat the wind. My no-teeth method is great for making a cast low to the water, not giving the wind an opportunity to alter the flight path of the net.

2. DO NOT PULL THE NET STRAIGHT UP - Once you have bait in your net, don't give them a chance to escape. You should retrieve

the net at a 45-degree angle or greater to you. If you are positioned directly above the opened net and pull it straight up or vertically, many of the baits can swim straight down and out of the net. By contrast, if you retrieve the net at an angle, you create the "bag" that the cast net was designed to form, which I've mentioned in this course. When I'm on the boat and if I find myself right on top of the net, I go to the helm and cut the wheel away from the net before I pull on the braille lines to provide that very angle to the net. Don't worry about the baits for the brief period of time it takes to change the angle. They are trapped inside the net and not going anywhere.

3. DO NOT TIE THE HANDLINE TO YOUR WRIST – When placing the cast net's handline around your wrist to begin the loading process, NEVER cinch the loop at the end of the handline over your hand on down your wrist. Should you cast your net and it gets caught in the trolling motor or something worse, you NEED the loop to come right off your wrist with ease. Keep the rope loose! I'd rather you lose your cast net than risk your life or a limb. I know professional mates that keep a dive knife on their leg or on a lanyard just in case of such a situation. I have had many close calls as well. Please keep it loose!

4. DO NOT THROW A LARGER NET THAN YOU CAN HANDLE - I love how my students are eager to challenge themselves to upgrade from six- and eight-foot nets to master ten, twelve and fourteen-footers. But you really must ask yourself whether you need a much larger net. Most of my students will need nothing larger than an all-purpose, eight-foot cast net. I'd rather you "pancake" an eight-footer nine out of ten times than to struggle to consistently open a twelve-foot cast net.

5. DO NOT CELEBRATE CHRISTMAS IN JULY - It's inevitable. One day you will throw on baits too small for the mesh size of your

net. We've warned you to avoid getting baits "gilled" in the mesh. We call this a "Christmas Tree." This occurs when the baits try to swim out of the net and they make it halfway out, getting their gills stuck in each mesh square of the net. Just about every square will have a baitfish stuck in it! It is a nightmare to clean out and will take you the better part of an hour. To avoid a Christmas tree, you must know your bait. In the summer here in Miami, we have pilchards off the beaches that are less than three inches. For that, we have a 1/4" net mesh designed specifically for small white baits. If we were to throw a 3/8" mesh, the baits would get gilled setting up Christmas in July.

Remember, fishing is a labor of love. And just because you have live bait doesn't mean you're automatically going to catch fish.

You'll need to work at it by putting out the perfect spread, swapping out weak baits for fresh baits, rigging, etc. Don't get me wrong. By catching your own live bait, the odds are stacked in your favor and I know you're going to get tight and catch more fish. Now, let's go fishing. Shall we?

Chapter 7
Let's Go Fishing

Congratulations! Now that you have mastered the art of cast netting and joined the *ten percent* club, you've earned a helping of "secret sauce" from Captain Mike!

I am confident I can count on you to use your cast net to its full potential now. Use these tips to not only help you find bait but do so faster and more efficiently.

It's time to go fishing…let's get started.

Look for the Signs

Catching bait is fun in its own right. I always tell my guests and clients on board to enjoy catching bait. Jokingly, I'll tell them that baitfish may be the only fish we see all day.

No matter the age or experience level of the angler, everyone has a hoot catching bait. And when you can make bait, expectations are high to catch fish, as they should be. It also engages everyone on board as they're now part of the team.

By now, you realize that much of my fishing success comes from having the freshest baits around. I plan my entire day -and many times my night - around catching bait. Many of my fishing trips will start well before sunrise to lock in the ideal tide or moon phase.

Under most circumstances, your best opportunity to catch bait will be in the early mornings, right at dawn. This is when birds will show you where the bait schools are hiding. Birds fish for a living and are far better bait fishermen than you and I will ever be. So, study their habits.

Once I'm on the water, I look and listen for the seagulls, pelicans, frigates, ospreys, etc., as they live on a baitfish diet and they rarely miss. Seeing even as few as just one gull is sometimes all it takes to put me on a school of bait. Often, you'll hear them screeching or whining as they seek a fresh meal - a sure sign that bait is nearby. And if you find the birds diving, it's go time!

While shadowing the birds, I'm constantly watching the surface of the water for movement and changes such as wakes, splashes, or "nervous water." The slightest trickle of a baitfish or flash of silver is all I need to grab my net and load up. Dusk and dawn are your best opportunities to see the baitfish on top as they are the most active then. Also be on the lookout for predators such as sharks, rays and dolphin as these are all signs of life and, more importantly, bait.

When you arrive in the area of the bait schools and begin "making bait", continue to pay attention to the surface of the water, birds and gamefish. If gamefish are exploding on the schools of baitfish, try not to make too much noise or ruckus. You could very well fish in the same spot so do your best not to shut down the bite going on around you.

Do yourself a favor: Buy a GREAT pair of polarized sunglasses. Polarized sunglasses reduce glare and allow your eyes to "see through" glare and the water itself. You are virtually blind without polarized sunglasses and you are placing yourself at a huge disadvantage. Reading the water will play into your success more than you realize.

We live in an age of amazing technology. You can combine what you see above the water's surface with sonar technology to see what's happening below the surface. Some of the best live bait fishermen I know rely heavily on their fish finders to enable them to catch bait at night so that they can sell baits to local fishermen at first light.

The same principles hold true if you're a freshwater angler, fishing lakes and backcountry waters. Gamefish such as largemouth bass can be seen aggressively striking the bait schools resembling raindrops on the surface - a telltale sign of bait concentrations. Shad and shiners make excellent live baits and you can make quick work of them with your newly-mastered cast net skills.

Now, you have a better idea of the signs for which to keep a lookout. When fishing with others, I seem to be the first person to spot a bird, dolphin or something that could help us "make bait." My head is continually "on a swivel" until I find the baits. I can't eat or drink until I make bait. I treat each bait trip as a fight for survival. It's make bait or go home.

Using Sonar to Find the Bait

For finding bait, you have an effective technological tool at your disposal: Sonar. Sonar uses sound waves to enable you to "see" what's underneath the boat. Sonar transmits sound pulses and interprets the returning sound waves or "echoes" to create a picture on the sonar display. The display can show you depth, bottom features such as wrecks and even schools of fish.

Marine electronics manufacturers are constantly improving sonar technology to help us find fish, including the recent development of CHIRP and side-scanning technology. If you have bought a fish finder/depth finder in the past five years, you likely have all you need to find bait schools beneath your boat. I don't recommend one depth finder brand over another brand because, quite honestly, most leading marine electronics brands offer depth finders that will serve you well. All that I ask is that you read the device's manual and spend time on the water learning how to use all of the device's features to zero in on your targeted baits.

Stay tuned for my upcoming Fish Finders Mastery Series. In the meantime, let me show you how I learned to make the most out of my fish finders/depth finders:

Let's go back to my friend Matt. If you recall, Matt introduced me to Live Bait fishing back in high school, the good ole 90s. Matt was a master at reading his fish finder to locate the baits like a *ten percenter*. Matt was an outdoorsman who fully embraced technology – very unique at the time. Matt realized that his best shot to make bait was to utilize his finder. Matt often fished a channel where the baits would hold in depths as much as forty feet at times, so he needed to "mark" the bait schools to catch them.

What's ironic is that Matt owned one of the cheapest depth finders that money could buy. Since the device's manual was very basic, Matt basically had to learn how to use the unit on the fly. Even though the unit featured a tiny four-inch screen with crummy resolution, Matt was amazing in his ability to discern bait balls from the rest of the readings. I can still hear Matt yelling from the helm, "They are behind the boat, drop now, twenty-five feet!" Sure enough, we would drop our Sabikis down to twenty-five feet and get crushed with a stringer of six beautiful baits every time. That's how I learned to use depth finders.

Again, I've found that the best way to learn the features of your finder is to get out on the water and USE the darn thing.

When showing students how to use a depth finder, I first instruct them to locate bait schools visually. Diving birds and feeding gamefish make it that much easier. As we motor up to the activity, we will inevitably see multicolored balls or blotches that indicate the school of baits. With just a bit of practice, my students will be able to discern whether the marks are bait or predators.

When it comes to reading a depth finder, let's consider an example of what separates the Pros from the Joes:

Just because I mark a good school of bait on my finder doesn't mean that I will throw my net immediately. I'm looking for the densest school possible. I'm going to stay patient and survey the surrounding water to see if I can find a school that fills the entire screen. This is the "one and done" zone and I've found my target. The Pros are patient.

Here is another situation:

Oftentimes two different bait species can be mixed in with each other. Threadfin herring, for example, will stay in the middle or on top of the water column while the pilchards are holding near the bottom. My preferred cast net baits of the two species are pilchards as pilchards are heartier baits and survive much longer than Threadfin Herring when caught with a cast net. I must carefully watch my fish finder until the "threads" are out of the way and the bottom is full of pilchards. That is when I strike!

It's a Team Effort

There are no free rides when you fish with Capt. Mike. If you come aboard, I am putting you to work! When I'm catching bait, I engage everyone aboard to pitch in and catch baits not only to teach them how to catch bait but because we can catch baits much quicker...and get fishing! Furthermore, if I can train my anglers how to read the depth finder, I can load up my cast net and head up to the bow to get ready to throw. As my students see the big red marks on the screen, they can shout them out to me, just like Matt used to do. Of course, I'm not solely relying on my anglers to put me on the bait. If the water is shallow and clear enough, I'm also looking for the bait on top or moving along the bottom. Having additional hands on deck never hurts when bait fishing and it's more fun for everyone.

Doing It All

On the days when I'm fishing solo - a one-man band – catching bait can be quite a challenge. I must remain at the helm to steer as well as, you guessed it, scrutinize the scrolling display of the depth finder. Once I find the bait, I must position the boat, preferably upwind, with enough lead time to clear and load the cast net in time to open up on the school.

Being able to read your sonar machine will tilt the scales in your favor when it comes to catching bait. The Pros are adept at reading a depth finder display, regardless of make, model or age of the machine. They know what the targeted baitfish look like on their screen, thanks to the countless hours spent on the water reading a slew of different depth finders.

So, when using your depth finder, break out your notebook to take notes or take screenshots with your phone and analyze your data. It won't be long before you can become proficient at reading depth finders.

Using Chum

Chum can be a bait fisherman's best friend...aside from birds, your depth finder or having Captain Mike aboard your boat.

Chum is ground up fish that is typically formed into the shape of a rectangular "block" and then frozen. A block of chum is placed into a mesh bag or special box and dropped into the water, behind the boat. As the chum block thaws, it releases the scent, oil and pieces of the ground-up fish. When your boat is on the anchor or even on the drift, chum is an effective way to attract baits such as pilchards, greenies and ballyhoo. The baits get lured right up to the transom and well within range of your cast net.

If you are new to bait fishing, go out to your local tackle shop and purchase two boxes of chum and a chum bag. Anchor up to where you typically see birds diving near a grass flat, channel marker, buoy, etc. Take the chum block out of the cardboard packaging – yes, this is going to be messy and smelly - and place the chum block into the chum bag. Cinch the chum block closed and secure the bag to a stern cleat. Then, just be patient and give it some time. You will need some current for this to work.

Once the bait shows up, let them get comfortable in your chum slick and let them get comfortable within range of your net (this is where your practicing comes in – you'll know what your effective range will be). Then, make your throw. Don't toss too early as the baits aren't leaving your free buffet anytime soon.

How to Find Bait Spots

Live bait fishermen are extremely secretive. It's for good reason. They have worked hard to dial in the bait after years of waking up early or staying out all night and identifying the seasons and conditions that make them successful in bait fishing. You will have to do the same if you want to maintain your *ten percent club* membership.

Forget about asking for bait spots. Instead, start by waking up early and getting started with the sun. Most baitfish species will be active in the early mornings and the birds will give away their locations. Keep in mind that most birds around bodies of water are on a 100% fish diet. They must catch baitfish to survive. Whether you are fishing lakes, piers, inlets, bays, etc., study the birds and you should find the bait.

You can also work the last few hours of daylight, just before the sun goes down. I have enjoyed a great deal of success finding baits in the evenings after work. Usually, I'll get in a solid hour of catching bait just as it's getting dark. The night is an incredible time to be a bait fisherman.

The more you go, the more you'll know. Once you identify and log trends, you'll know exactly where to find baits regardless of the season, tide, temperature, etc. By now you know what to look for, you just need to put in the time and effort.

Seasons and Behavior of Live Bait

Looking back at my many years spent on the water, it's never ceased to amaze me how the seasons affect the location and behavior of the various bait species that I target. Oftentimes, the behavior and density of the bait schools would tell me which season has arrived.

All summer long, catching bait is easy around here. Well, for me anyway. I know that from early June through the end of August, I will have no problem loading my livewells with small to medium-sized white baits - and usually with just one cast. I know exactly where they will be and which cast net to throw: I'll break out my 1/4" mesh net, so as not to gill the smaller baits. I learned my lesson from "Christmas Trees" that 3/8" mesh is simply too big for these baits.

As the summer starts to wind down and fall is in the air, my "spider senses" tingle: The fall season is upon us and migrating baitfish will soon clog inshore and nearshore waters.

Years of experience and long days on the water have introduced me to the seasonal patterns to anticipate and to prepare for them accordingly. It's almost second nature to anticipate where the bait will be, how I will catch them and how I will turn them into trophy catches.

Whether you are targeting shrimp, crabs, shad, mullet, greenies, or bunker - the seasons are trying to tip you off. Mother Nature is speaking to you, so listen.

Live bait abundance is seasonal and studying the habits of live bait will make you a better fisherman, without a doubt. The *ten percenters* use the seasons to know exactly where to go, what to look for and which net to use during each of the seasons. The *ten percenters* have mapped out the seasonal trends and can stay ahead of the Joes who do not make the effort to gather such valuable data.

A great example of a seasonal bait migration is the "Mullet Run," which is a phenomenon that occurs every fall in Southeast Florida. This is one of the most epic bait migrations in the world. As summer ends and temperatures drop, millions of mullet travel south, down the Florida coast along the beaches and down the Intracoastal Waterway, leveraging safety in numbers as predators such as tarpon, sharks, bluefish, and big snook are waiting to ambush the massive schools.

Beginning September 1st every year, I switch gears and start scanning the beaches and inshore waters, hoping to detect the early signs of this great phenomenon. The schools of mullet appear along the beach as massive, dark clouds resembling oil slicks. It's one and done time! Making bait doesn't get much easier than during this migration. The bonus is that, once you load up on mullet, you can fish the same spot as the predators are lurking along the periphery of the massive schools.

This phenomenon, like clockwork, occurs annually. However, mother nature doesn't want to make it easy on us. Year to year, the mullet run never starts on the same day and the duration of the run varies as well. Yes, making bait is fairly easy but you still need to be a *ten percenter* to take full advantage of this migration.

It's the same for my friends to the north. As winter turns to spring, the ice melts, cast nets are removed from their winter storage and ready to work - make bait.

Take New York, for example. Striper fishermen await the return of the menhaden, known locally as "Bunker." There are days when the bunker are plentiful and easy to net. Local fishermen often use snag hooks to catch bunker one-at-a-time but there is no better way to catch fresh bunker unharmed than with a cast net. Since New York regulations limit cast nets to a maximum size of ten feet, the Pros utilize cast nets that are built to ten feet, with large mesh and heavy leadlines for fast sink rates.

Changes in water temperature and wind can trigger bait migrations and spawning behavior. Identifying these acts of mother nature can greatly enhance your cast netting success. Studying the seasons and identifying the patterns of baitfish is what separates the Pros from the Joes. I'm not saying that you must dedicate your life to baitfish. I just want you to constantly be learning and improving.

At times, I don't know whether to be proud or embarrassed at how much I know about a baitfish. But it's in my best interest to learn and absorb all that I can and to capitalize on the seasonal behaviors of live bait.

I'm driven to catch so much bait that there are times when I can barely lift my net over the gunnels and just maybe, do some live chumming.

Live Chumming for Big Game Fish

"Why so much bait, Captain Mike?" "Do we have enough bait yet, Captain Mike?" "What are you going to do with all that bait...Captain Mike?"

I hear these questions all the time from clients, students and fishing buddies. My answer is ALWAYS: It's never enough!

My clients and students are always so intrigued and, at times, shocked to see me hoist over the gunnel a cast net loaded with hundreds of baitfish and dump them into my livewell. Guess what? That's not enough. *It's never enough.*

I repeat the process again and again until each livewell is "blacked out." Blacked out is a term we use when the clear water in your well appears to be black from being packed with bait.

The appeal of cast netting to me is the ability to catch an immense amount of bait in the shortest amount of time. It is a feeling of Zen when I'm content with the amount of bait I have.

Even though I load up on bait, I do not catch so much bait as to be wasteful or to abuse this natural resource. There is also a point of diminishing returns as you will lose some baits if you overwhelm your livewell's ability to refresh the water and remove waste.

Once we top-off the livewells, it's time to go fishing. Whether we are going inshore or offshore, the real fun begins now: Live Chumming. Live Chumming is the technique of releasing live baitfish (we call them "freebies") around the boat so that they can swim freely – no hooks – and entice predators into your spread. The baitfish will scatter frantically around the boat, sending out vibrations that your target species can sense and are compelled to come closer to investigate.

More often than not, the baitfish you release into the water will school up and swim away attracting predators. Your target species pick up on the vibrations and will proceed to attack the baits that have separated from the school – these are the baits that are part of your spread and have hooks in them.

Live chumming produces some of the most incredible and exciting fishing you can experience. If all goes well, you create your own feeding frenzy that is amazing to watch. Predators will violently feed, exploding on the "freebies" and it won't be long until they find your lines - Fish on!

Pro Tip: Do not overfill your bait well. By now, you can probably catch more live bait than most, however, if you put too many baits in one well, they will all die. For baits such as thread-fin herring, I use the rule of 1 gallon of water per bait. That is fifty baits in my fifty-gallon well.

Take Care of Your Bait

Here is another critical detail that the Joes overlook: Take care of your baits
– to the point of obsession. Think about it: You've been diligent and
worked very hard to load up your livewells with live baits that nothing can
resist. Would you just toss those baits on the deck to let them die? Of course
not!

One striking difference I see between the Pros and the Joes is the lengths to
which the Pros will go to ensure that their baits remain happy and healthy
once inside their wells. The Pros leave nothing to chance to keep their baits
alive and well. This is a logical extension to the art of cast netting.

Here are my top five tips for storing and handling your bait:

➤ **Water Flow:**

The fresher and cleaner the water, the healthier and more robust your live
baits will be. A continuous flow of fresh water (by "fresh," I mean "new,
clean water") into your livewell and overflowing at the top is the easiest and
most effective setup to accomplish. Simply use an external bait pump to
bring in fresh water and DO NOT turn it off until you are back to the
dock. Keep it running continuously while holding live baits. Some Pros will
go a step further and add multiple inflows to ensure there are no dead zones
- areas of low oxygen or no oxygen.

If you are storing bait in a bucket such as crabs, shrimp or white bait, a
battery-powered "bubbler" works great. However, I make it a point to
change out the water every thirty minutes and I try not to overload the
bucket with baits.

➤ **Capacity:**

Rarely will I see Joes overloading their livewells because they're simply not able to catch enough baits to make this an issue. However, now that you've become a *ten percenter*, you'll have to worry about this "first world" problem. Knowing how much bait you can hold in the healthiest condition possible will be critical to your fishing success.

I prefer at least one fifty-gallon livewell along my boat's center of gravity. If I'm holding all big baits, I use the rule of one gallon of water per bait. This means I can only hold fifty baits and no more. If I am catching smaller baits, I can double that figure.

My boat is configured with three livewells. I use them strategically: the "select" baits are placed in the spacious fifty-gallon livewell described above. This is the penthouse. This is where my best baits will be pampered. These baits will enjoy a ratio of one gallon of water per bait and I'll fish them first to increase my chances at a quick bite. I'll devote my forward livewell to my live chummers. My aft livewell will supplement my fifty-gallon livewell. With multiple livewells, I can also store baits by species. This way I'm not looking for that sole mullet in a well full of pilchards. Multiple livewells also provide redundancy in case I lose a livewell pump while I'm out fishing – and pumps DO fail at the least opportune time. Take it from me.

> **Bait Checks:**

A-B-C: Always **B**e Checking. I obsessively check and recheck the condition of my baits to ensure proper waterflow and pump operation. You never know when a pump might quit on you or when a clump of seaweed blocks the pickup. Be looking for anything and everything.

My head is constantly on a swivel and I treat my baits like newborn children. I will slow down as I approach a big wave on the way out or plot a course that is not as choppy to avoid beating up the baits as they slosh within the livewell. If I notice a bait that looks ill or has lost scales, I remove it ASAP. When one baitfish dies, it "teaches" the other baits how to die. It's contagious. Remove that bait immediately!

> **Handling Baits:**

When it's time to get baits out, I use a custom bait "dip" net with a soft mesh as to not scrape or "scale" the bait. You can get one on livebait.com. It's another very small detail but remember what I said - it's the little things.

I scoop baits out of the livewell one-at-a-time. ONE-BAIT-AT-A-TIME! If I grabbed more than one in each scoop, those baits would rub against each other and return to the livewell with their protective "slime" compromised. These baits won't last very long and you can forget about bringing them back to the dock to drop into your bait pen. ONE-BAIT-AT-A-TIME.

Nothing irks me more than when I ask my crew to hand me a bait and he scoops out a dozen baits, then hands me the net. Especially when he knows better! Now, YOU know better too.

➢ Be Quick About It

When I'm putting a fresh live bait on the hook, I do so as quickly as possible. There is no reason to handle a bait more than five seconds. Get that bait on the hook and over the side ASAP. We want the friskiest live bait possible, which represents a natural bait to predators.

These five tips will help you present the liveliest and heartiest live baits possible and will maximize the blood, sweat and tears you expended to catch those baits in the first place. Be obsessive. Be meticulous. Be fanatical. It will all pay off when you bring that trophy catch alongside the boat.

If you think I'm nitpicking with these five tips, then you had better go back to the beginning of this Mastery Series. But I'm pretty sure you are with me and understand: It's all about the bait. It's always been about the bait.

I have fished with some of the best live bait fishermen and they are all neurotic with their bait. You should be too. It's a common trait of the *ten percenters*.

CHAPTER 8
CAST NET CARE

Cast Net Maintenance

As with all your fishing gear, the better you take care of your cast net, the better it will take care of you. A premium cast net can be a significant investment – you need to take good care of it just like the *ten percenters*.

After each trip, you must remove any baitfish or debris from the mesh that you may have overlooked when using the net. Don't forget to check the braille lines and leadlines.

Next, hose off the net with fresh water and air dry. **You can hang up the net, however, DO NOT hang the net with the leads off the ground.** This will stretch out the monofilament in your braille lines and ruin the net.

A perfectly clean net sets you up for your next bait session. I can't tell you how often I accidentally left baitfish in the net, only to start my day off with the pungent smell of decaying fish! It is now part of my routine to rinse, dry and store my net after every trip. I want to start the next trip with a fresh slate, a net free of twist, tangles, debris and baitfish.

You'll often see my cast nets draped all over my boat or even my yard while they are drying in preparation for my next trip.

The more you use your cast net, especially in saltwater, the more it may become rough or brittle to the touch. Cheap nets are notorious for feeling stale, rigid or brittle after saltwater use. Premium high-performance cast nets like a JuJu Cast Net are manufactured using the softest monofilament and shipped ready for use. However, after frequent use - especially in saltwater - you may want to occasionally soak the net in an environmentally-friendly fabric softener.

How To Store Your Cast Net

No matter the size of your boat, space is always at a premium. You only have so much room with which to work. After you've loaded up your livewells, you need to store your cast nets to protect both the nets and anyone else aboard. If you're like me, you want to get it out of the way when not in use. A clean deck makes me a happy captain and after I "make bait", I take the time to clean the net, give it a good rinse and store it out of the way. Nothing is more frustrating than constantly stepping over a net on deck or even worse, getting stray hooks tangled in the net when trying get the spread out. My investment paid off tenfold, in filling up my livewells and now it's time to properly store it for the next bait session.

Rinse the net as best you can and place it in an available hatch or storage area. If you have no storage available, clean the net, place it in a bucket and try to keep the bucket away from the action. It's important to keep the net clean. Do not store a net that is wet and dirty in confined spaces for long periods of time. You'll diminish the life of your net.

I have found the best place to store a wet net is in a designated plastic fish basket. It is very similar to a laundry basket. What's great about the basket is that you can place your net in the basket, hose it off and allow the net to breathe and dry. I carry these baskets on my boat and in my truck. They come in handy at times for many other things including dumping your baits from your cast net, storing anchors, etc. You can get them on <u>LiveBait.com</u>.

You'll see the Pros often leave their nets in these fish baskets, rather than storing them in hatches. It's because they are constantly on the bait grind and know a dirty net will do them no good at their next bait session. By rinsing them off and using fish baskets, the nets can breathe and dry properly. Join the *ten percenters* and use the basket too.

How to Repair a Cast Net

As a cast net fisherman, you will inevitably tear your net. It's going to happen. It's an awful feeling to get your net hung up on a rock or obstruction and pull up your net only to see gaping holes. It happens to the best of us and I'm a believer that if you do not blow up a net every now and then, you're not fishing hard enough.

Not too long ago, I was chasing mullet in murky water about five feet deep. I could see the mullet up on top but nothing below. I made the perfect throw and let the net sink. And to my disbelief, I threw directly on an old, abandoned crab trap covered in barnacles! Ugh! I pretty much destroyed the net and instead of repairing it, I had to get a new one. Over two hundred dollars down the drain! Remember when I said your net is an investment. Think about how many thousands of dollars I saved by not buying lures, live bait, etc. So, I'm OK with the occasional catastrophe, but it still stinks. I always hope to get at least one year out of my net and after that I'm winning, but sometimes mother nature has other plans.

Repairing a cast net correctly could get expensive. Oftentimes, repaired sections are weaker than the rest of the net or the repaired sections may affect how the net opens. Unless you're looking at a minor repair such as small holes, I recommend you stomach the loss and buy a new net. Turn your damaged net into your "who cares" net. Meaning it's the one you use around rocks, oyster bars, peculiar and new areas.

If you have small holes or a popped braille line, you can repair it, but be prepared for a big bill and in my experience, the net is just never the same.

When my cast nets get slightly damaged, I make them my "dirty work" or "disposable" nets. This is just like how I move my older t-shirts and pants to my "painting" and "yard work" clothes. The net can still catch bait. I will use these nets to target mullet over rocky areas or baitfish over oyster bars. If some bait gets out, I'm OK with that until I get a new net. It's my "who cares" net and I'm just happy I'm still able to get bait with it.

CHAPTER 9
SUMMARY

Conservation

If you made it this far and have practiced what I'm preaching, then you've made me proud. There are few things more rewarding than when a student "gets it." You have given me a great sense of accomplishment and for that, I truly thank you.

Before I followed this path, I had no clue that teaching would be this much fun and I have a newfound respect and gratitude for all the wonderful teachers out there.

Seeing so many of you outdoors, using your cast net to its full potential is exactly why I put so much time and effort into this series. We are "makin' bait" and we are the *ten percenters*. Ninety percent of fishermen envy us.

However, this Mastery Series would not be complete without a discussion of conservation and our obligation as responsible anglers. And while I trust you will use your newfound skill to catch bait in moderation, we must continue to protect our resources and fish responsibly.

While using a cast net is a sustainable way to catch baitfish as a recreational angler, let's not overdo it. I ask that we all practice conservation techniques by only taking what we need and releasing what we do not.

Remember when I told you how I learned how to catch live bait with my good friend Matt in the 90s? Well, those baits have not been in that same area for about twenty years now. Some say it is from overfishing. Others say that dredging, over-development or declining water quality are the culprits. Whatever the case may be, this particular bait resource is gone. And while

I have personally witnessed baitfish populations decline to the point of disappearing, we as *ten percenters* must continue to be dedicated custodians of our available resources.

A recreational cast net fisherman cannot put a dent in the baitfish populations. With the average cast net size net of 7 feet, the recreational harvest is a fraction of the pressure placed on bait populations by commercial harvesting operations. That being said, we must do our part. Some of the best fishermen I know will consciously catch ONLY the amount of the bait they need. They won't beat up their bait spots or abuse the resource. You should do the same. Without thriving baitfish, there are no game fish. When the baitfish disappear or thin out in the body of water you fish, there is no reason for the game fish to stick around.

By being conservation-minded, we preserve and may even improve for our future generations.

Teaching Kids

Few things in life can compare to passing your love of fishing and your knowledge to your son or daughter. I have been fortunate to teach kids of all ages to use cast nets from three-footers all the way to twelve-footers. Children are so eager to learn and their excitement is truly contagious. When my junior angler students catch their first fish, it brings me back to how excited I was when I started my angling journey all those years ago.

For kids aged 6 years and younger, I like to start them out with the El Niño series of JuJu cast nets. It is a three-foot cast net with plastic weights and comes in a cool little bucket with a fun Polynesian character logo, named Keanu. This net is very kid-friendly and the kids just love it.

I'll teach my younger students by going out to the lawn and placing little targets on the grass such as leaves and show them a variation of the "No

Teeth Method." Because the net is only three feet, the child only needs to split the net to load it. You'll be surprised at just how quickly they learn!

As my junior angler students grow bigger, I move them up to a six-foot net and then eventually to an eight or ten-footer. After that, they don't need ole' Captain Mike's help anymore. I also love it when teenage anglers show interest in the big nets that I'm throwing. It reminds me of when I was their age and watching the commercial bait guys pancake big nets and bring up loads of bait. I may be getting old but sharing and creating memories never will.

Why Purchase a Premium Net?

As a live bait fisherman for many years, I never found a cast net that "checked all of the boxes" for how I used them. Some nets were better in some aspects than others. I could never find a cast net manufacturer that could build the perfect net for me. So, I decided to build it myself and JuJu Tackle Company was born!

When I founded JuJu Tackle Company, I set out to build a high-performance cast net by marrying the highest-quality components with the best hand-made construction techniques. After countless hours of testing in real-bait scenarios, we've built the perfect cast net. From soft mesh webbing to heavier lead lines, we've scrutinized everything and created a series of nets that have to be approved by our most demanding customer and harshest critic: Me.

Have Fun

I hope this Mastery Course exceeded your expectations and will pay dividends throughout your fishing career. I have been using cast nets for thirty-five years and have been a hard-core live bait fisherman for the past twenty-five. When I started publishing how-to videos and began one-on-

one classes and seminars, I learned that so many anglers share my passion for catching bait. And those who didn't share that passion before watching my videos, certainly do now. I receive many videos and photos from students and viewers showing how well they can now toss pancakes. They are so proud and so am I. This means that I'm doing something right.

My mission is to share the joy of getting outdoors with our kids and future generation of anglers. I long to see them picking up a cast net for the first time, learning how to throw it, then getting outdoors and catch fish. I'm doing my best to embed conservation techniques into each lesson as well….and the future looks bright, indeed!

You don't have to thank me. This course was a lot of hard work. However, it was worth every second! Seeing you catch bait, smiling with your family and creating memories is more than I could ever dream of!

If you benefitted from this course and enjoyed it, there is one thing you can do for Ole Captain Mike. As an author, our lifeblood is positive reviews. Positive reviews spread the word that this book was worthwhile and it validates the many hours of blood, sweat and tears that I've poured into this labor of love. Therefore, if you enjoyed this course, please leave an online review. I sincerely appreciate it.

Now, get out there, go have some fun and **Make Bait!**

Tight Lines and Great Fishing,

Captain Mike

ABOUT THE AUTHOR

Captain Michael Grimm is an author, conservationist and entrepreneur with a passion to convey to fellow anglers the tips and tricks learned over thirty years of angling. He's helped thousands improve their fishing skills through his YouTube channel - ReelReports. He is a United States Coast Guard certified charter captain.

CERTIFICATION QUIZ
QUESTIONS

To complete your cast net certification, you must score a 70%. Good luck. You've got this!

1. What's the component of a cast net featuring lines of monofilament attached to the swivel that run directly through the horn and down to the lead line.

A) Hand Line

B) Selvage

C) Lead Line

D) Braille Lines

2. If you were catching large mullet in five feet of water, which of the following is the best cast net for the job?

A) 5ft, 1/4"mesh

B) 8ft, 3/16" mesh

C) 12ft, 1/4" mesh

D) 10ft, 1" mesh

3. Which of the following affects the sink rate of a cast net?

A) The length of the net

B) The weight of the net

C) The mesh size of the net

D) All of the above

4. The loop of the handline should be extremely tight around your wrist so it does not fall off.

- (True)

- (False)

5. When selecting a cast net, which of the following is the most important consideration?

A) Color of Net

B) Mesh Size of Net

C) Bucket Size

D) None of the above

~ 119 ~

6. When throwing a cast net in windy conditions, it is best to throw with the wind.

- ▪ (True)

- ▪ (False)

7. If you had to have one cast net to do it all, what would be the best option?

A) 14ft, 1/2" Mesh

B) 3ft, 3/8" Mesh

C) 8ft, 3/8" Mesh

D) 5ft, 1/4" Mesh

8. When cleaning a net, it is best to hang the net completely in the air with the leads off the ground.

- ▪ (True)

- ▪ (False)

9. Using the triple load to throw a cast net, which of the following is true:

    A) Throw as hard as you can to get the best pancake.

    B) Do a spin to get momentum to open the net.

    C) Use the centrifugal force of the leads to propel the net open.

    D) Put the lead line in your teeth.

10. What is the number one indicator that there is bait around:

    A) Birds are diving in the area

    B) Other bait fishermen are in the area

    C) Game fish are blowing up baitfish

    D) All of the above

11. When wading with a cast net, you should:

    A) Carry the net high and out of the water

    B) Load the net after getting in the water

    C) Make plenty of noise as to scare the school

    D) Wade as fast as you can, stealth is not necessary.

12. If targeting ballyhoo (8" baitfish) on the reef, which is the best cast net to yield the most bait with one throw:

A) 3 ft, 3/8" mesh

B) 6 ft, 1" mesh

C) 8 ft, 3/8" mesh

D) 5 ft, 1/4" mesh

13. When using the triple load method, if the net doesn't open up fully on the lower left side, what is the cause:

A) You didn't throw the net hard enough

B) You loaded too much net over your shoulder

C) You didn't hold the lead line in your pinky long enough

D) None of the above

14. When coiling up your handline from your cast net, it is best to:

A) Tie the rope off to a cleat on your boat

B) Tie the rope to your wrist as tight as possible so you don't lose it

C) Place the loop around your wrist loosely so it may come off easily in case of an accident

D) Ask a friend to hold the end of the rope while you throw

15. Which of the following statements is false:

A) A cast net is a sustainable device to catch baitfish

B) 1/4" mesh is good for baits from 1" to 3"

C) You cannot catch 10" baits with 3/8" mesh

D) You do not have to be big and strong to throw a cast net

16. To throw a cast net as far as you can, you should:

A) Do a spin to generate momentum

B) Get a running start

C) Grip the cast net lower, closer to your knee and do a full shoulder turn to generate more momentum.

D) Work out more

17. If your cast net gets stuck on the bottom or a structure, you should NOT

A) Try to pull up from the opposite side you threw on

B) Cut the line and leave the cast net in the water

C) Do short gentle tugs to see if you can release the snagged area.

D) If shallow enough, go into the water to try to release by hand

18. When throwing a cast net on a windy day and you cannot throw with the wind, you should

A) Throw the net as low as you can to the water

B) Try to find an area that is diagonal to the wind, rather than throwing directly into it

C) Make shorter throws

D) All of the above

19. In Texas, a cast net may not have a diameter greater than fourteen-feet. When you go to the store, which size cast net will be your best option?

A) 14Ft, 3/8 Mesh

B) 8Ft, 3/8 Mesh

C) 7Ft, 3/8 Mesh

D) 10Ft, 3/8 Mesh

20. When targeting mullet, you come upon a creek that is fifteen feet deep in the middle, with shallow banks along the edges. You see a large school out in the middle and a medium-size school up on the shallow banks in about 2 feet of water. You are throwing an 8-foot, 3/8 inch mesh net. Which of the following is your best opportunity at yielding the most bait in one throw?

A) Throw on the large school over and over.

B) Stalk the bait in shallow water and throw on the medium size school first.

C) Wait for the medium school on the bank to join the big school in deep water.

D) None of the above

Answer Key

1.D 2.D 3.D 4.F 5.B 6.F 7.C 8.F 9.C 10.D 11.A 12.C 13.B
14.C 15.C 16.C 17.B 18.D 19.C 20.B

INDEX

Made in the USA
Middletown, DE
10 September 2024

60129148R00086